Hands-On Geography

Easy and Fun Activities for Exploring God's World

by Maggie S. Hogan

Cover Design by Christy Shaffer

Layout by Ivy Ulrich-Bonk

Hands-On Geography
Easy & Fun Activities for Exploring God's World

Library of Congress Catalog Card Number: 2001116602
ISBN 10: 1-892427-03-6
ISBN 13: 978-1-892427-03-8

Copyright 1994 Margaret S. Hogan
Revised Edition copyright 2001

Published by:
BRIGHT IDEAS PRESS
P.O. Box 333
Cheswold, DE 19936
www.BrightIdeasPress.com

ACKNOWLEDGMENTS

I'd like to thank the Delaware families who assisted us
by "field-testing" many of the ideas in this book.
Their suggestions and comments were a terrific help!
Appels, Bakers, Hathcocks, Lawrences, Rakes, Smiths, and Woods.

Also, my thanks go to:
Bob Hogan -- for writing the Bible study on Joseph's Journey.
Tyler Hogan -- for providing the outstanding maps.
Celeste Rakes and Muriel Van Wave -- for their many contributions.

Dedicated to:
Janice Baker, my sister in Christ, co-hort in adventure,
and the original co-author of the first *Hands-On Geography*.
*"Thanks dear! We've been through so much together
-- and most of it was my fault!"*

INTRODUCTION

Geography -- this vital subject, once heavily emphasized in early American education is now, too often, neglected. We are, as a nation, geographically illiterate. We've all read horror stories of students who were unable to identify the United States on a map of the world or to name the ocean off the coast of California. In my travels, I've heard more stories about adults who are equally dismal in their geographic knowledge.

As Christians, isn't it incumbent upon us to teach our children about God's world around us? How are we, or they, going to be witnesses to the ends of the Earth if we can't even find our way there! Of course, geography isn't just the location of places. Economics, politics, science, religion, and culture are all affected by, and intertwined with, geography. For us to impact the world for Christ we need to be aware of our world, now more than ever.

Political events and social issues can best be understood in the context of history and geography. Informed citizens wanting to be Christ's ambassadors need to understand from where we come as well as something about the world around us.

This book contains ideas, teaching tips, reproducibles, projects, and resources for teaching geography throughout the elementary years. Browse through and then pick a few activities to do. There is not a certain order in which they should be done, although some of the map projects are more advanced than others. The idea is to begin somewhere and then remember to teach geography on a regular basis, realizing that geography can often be easily included in history, science, and even literature. Look for ideas that are appealing to you, that have relevance to your child's interests, or significance to other courses you're teaching.

Besides specific geography activities, many of the ideas in this book include history, science, literature, and art. The Five Themes of Geography are included, along with some teaching ideas for explaining each theme. Perhaps the National Geography Bee would be good motivation for your family; don't miss the chapter on preparing for the Bee. A section on timelines is included because, after all, everything happens sometime as well as someplace. In the back of the book you'll find a wealth of outline maps, vocabulary words, and resources.

I hope this book is a great beginning to a lifelong geographic adventure! Now is the best time to be motivated and encouraged to teach this important subject!

Blessings,

Maggie Hogan

TABLE OF CONTENTS

The National Geography Bee

What is the first thing you think of when you hear the word geography? Maps? Globes? States and Capitals? There is so much more to geography, though! Here is a definition worth thinking about, provided by the National Geographic Society:

A knowledge of place names, location of cultural and physical features, distribution and patterns of languages, religions, economic activities, population and political systems. Physical regions and physical phenomena, such as tectonic activity, land form, climate, bodies of water, soils and flora and fauna. The changes in places and areas through time, including how people have modified the environment. Cartographers' tools, such as maps, instruments, graphs and statistics, are also a part of geography.

Whew! That covers a lot of territory! Geography is such a large subject -- it can seem overwhelming. Just remember that you naturally cover a lot of geographic concepts within your other curriculum, especially history and science. The important point here is to be aware of what geography is and to make a concentrated effort to consciously spend time on it. You might want to focus on a different aspect of geography each year. Additionally,

make a habit of using reference materials and maps, discussing current events, and actively noticing geographic topics in daily life. This will go a long way toward learning geography.

For some, it helps to have a goal for earnestly pursuing geographic literacy. The National Geography Bee (NGB) provides just such a motivation. This event is an objective to work towards. Along the way you'll probably find that the journey itself is great fun!

How do you participate in the NGB? Principals or Directors of U.S. schools (and homeschool support groups) with students in grades four through eight must register their schools to participate in the National Geography Bee before the early fall deadline. Principals may request registration by writing on school letterhead. Registration has been about $30.00. Check to see what the fee is this year. Send the letter to the address below.

Materials are mailed to registered schools in November.

National Geography Bee
National Geographic Society
1145 17th Street N.W.
Washington, DC 20036-4688

There must be a minimum of six students in grades fourth, fifth, sixth, seventh, or eighth grades in order for your group to participate. (The six students may be in any combination of these grade levels.)

The NGB occurs in three stages, beginning at the school level. School level bees must take place between specific dates in December and January. Each school winner takes a written test, and the top hundred scorers in each state and territory compete at the state level in April. The winner of each state level bee proceeds to the national competition.

The 55 state and territory winners meet at the National Geographic Society headquarters in Washington, D.C., for the national competition in May. The contestants compete for the first place prize of a $25,000 college scholarship. The second-and third-place winners receive $15,000 and $10,000 scholarships, respectively. *Jeopardy!* host Alex Trebek moderates the final rounds.

Homeschoolers are making a great showing in the Bee each year. The 1999 National Geography Bee Winner was 13-year-old David Beihl, a home-educated student from South Carolina! He won the $25,000 college scholarship!

How to Prepare for the Bee

Preparing is half the fun! There are so many interesting things to learn about our world. Read, read, and read some more! Cozy up with atlases, peruse almanacs, and digest the newspaper! (*God's World* publications are also good for current events.) National Geographic puts out a monthly magazine called *National Geographic World*. This is a great resource for Bee preparation. Even if you don't subscribe, your student will find it at the library or on-line at www.nationalgeographic.com.

Obviously you can not teach everything in one year. Pick an area of detailed study and supplement with general reading. For the bee, it's always wise to spend some time on the United States. Students should know their states and capitals, major geographic features and regions, major rivers and lakes, and something of our products and people. Additionally, remember to teach maps, charts, and graphs reading and interpreting skills.

See *Recommended Resources* in the back of this book for great geography materials!

In Delaware, the 1997 state winner was a homeschooled student named Domini Oguinake. The *Delaware News-Journal* ran an article about the NGB including a picture of Domini praying before a round! In an interview with him, the reporter asked Domini if his mother taught him everything he knows. Domini, 11, said "No, but she taught me how to study so I'd know everything I know."

Let's give our kids the tools they need to be life-long independent learners!

Do the Bee!!

Advice for Support Group NGB Directors:

1. Hold a short mock bee to introduce students to the bee format.

2. Obtain three volunteers to be timer, score keeper, and moderator.

    A. Moderator: It is preferable if the moderator does not have a student participating, but it's permissible if he/she does. The moderator should read over the questions a few days before the bee in order to be familiar with the procedures and with the questions. Some of those words can be tricky to pronounce!

    B. The Timer and Scorekeeper should have a clear understanding of the procedures. Make up your own score sheets ahead of time.

3. Some homeschool groups prefer there be no siblings at the bee. If they are present, they need to be kept quiet. (In all fairness, it's more often parents who are whispering, not the siblings!) During the rounds, the rooms must remain absolutely quiet so that all students have a fair chance to concentrate without distractions.

4. Make copies of NGB Certificates to award after the bee. You might like to give small tokens to all participants -- globe key-rings or erasers and the like. You may ask a business to furnish appropriate prizes.

5. Be prepared to take pictures and fill out the publicity information to send to your local newspaper, announcing your bee winners.

Chapter 1
Homemade Games

Making homemade games is an appealing way to learn more about geography. Why make board games? Game making is an excellent learning activity for many reasons:

A. Students use higher level thinking skills:

      1. what's the purpose of the game?
      2. what are the rules?
      3. what is the strategy?
      4. long range planning
      5. board design

B. The research adds depth and breadth to a subject.
C. The "fun factor" provides motivation for study.
D. Games are great pre-study interest builders or post-studies retention checkers.

Games can range from simple memory or "go fish"-type games to more complex problem-solving games or fact-finding games. It helps to start with simpler games before moving on to the more difficult. It is easiest to begin with assigning the type game they are to make -- using a familiar and easy-to-play game as the model, for example "Memory," "Bingo," or "Candy Land."

How do you actually do this? This chapter includes tips and hints as well as a couple of sample game ideas to get those creative juices flowing. Use these as a jumping off point. Kids love the opportunity to make rules, exert some decision-making control, and play all at the same time!

Tip
Where do I find pieces to use? Buy old board games at yard sales for $1.00 and save them for game-making time. Scavenge for spinners, dice, marks, boards, and any other cool pieces. Forget the rules and save just the good stuff. Dump the works into a big "game box" and now the kids have a ready assortment of pieces to use in building their next game... Or, check under the couch...

What about rules?
Rule making can be problematic. Major tip: play it in stages as it is being designed to check for rule problems. It's very frustrating to spend lots of time on a game and then find out as you're playing it that the rules just don't work. Part of the challenge, of course, is creating simple and workable rules. That's way modeling a game after existing games is preferable for the elementary crowd.

How much time?
Allow more time than you think you need! Game Day might mean setting aside a whole day or two to work on the game while the enthusiasm runs high. If you can't do that, then certainly allow four or five afternoons to finish the project.

HOMEMADE GAME #1
Memory

Materials

- ◆ (Two of each) Pictures or postcards from country of choice
- ◆ 3 x 5 index cards
- ◆ Glue stick
- ◆ Contact paper (optional -- for durability)

Directions

1. Either:
   collect two of everything or
   make one photocopy of each picture or use one picture and its written name
   (a picture of a prairie and the word "prairie").
2. Glue each picture onto an index card.
3. Cover with contact paper, if desired.

To Play

Shuffle cards and lay them face down on a table in rows. Each child takes a turn picking up a card, then picking up another that they hope is a match. If they get a match they keep that pair, if they don't get a match they put both cards back face down in the same place. The player with the most matches when all the cards are paired, wins.

This game is good for learning states & capitals, geography vocabulary, etc.

You can also use these cards to play "Go Fish."

HOMEMADE GAME #2
Destination Egypt (Or any other country!)

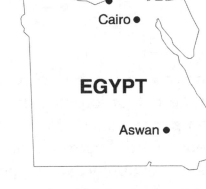

Alexandria •
Cairo •
EGYPT
Aswan •

Materials
* Encyclopedia
* Other reference material on Egypt
* 3 x 5 index cards
* Poster board and markers
* Game materials from your game box (spinner or dice, tokens to use for movement)

Directions

Help students develop 10-20 questions about Egypt. If playing with a wide age range, make some questions easy, some hard, and label them thus. Write answers to the questions on the back of the card. Use questions that can be answered easily in just a few words. If more than one child is working on this game, ask them not to share answers until game time.

After they have a stack of questions written, design a game board using something about Egypt in its layout: designed in the shape of a pyramid or drawn in the shape of the Nile, etc. Have a "start" and a "stop" or "end" spaces on the board.

After the game board is finished, work together to decide the rules of the game.* (Simple is better!)

* This process may seem backwards, but if they write the rules first they're often so complicated it takes forever to design a board to match them.

HOMEMADE GAME #3
Tara's "Mummy-Go"

Tara, 9, designed a game to play when learning vocabulary words about Ancient Egypt. She made four large cards in the shape of pyramids out of 11 x 17 construction paper, called "Mummy-Go cards." She drew an even number of boxes on each card. She randomly wrote vocabulary words into each box. Then she took each vocabulary word and wrote it on a 3 x 5 index card called a "Pharaoh card." On the flip side she wrote the definition in the form of a question. "What is the term for the way Egyptians watered their crops?" Answer "irrigation." Then, for fun, she drew little hieroglyphic shapes onto small circles of paper to use for markers.

To play the game, each person gets a Mummy-Go card and a handful of hieroglyph chips. The Reader draws a Pharaoh card and reads it aloud. Whoever answers the question correctly AND has that vocabulary word on his card, gets to put a hieroglyph chip onto the space with the correct word. When someone has five chips in a row, they can call out, "Mummy-Go!" and win the game.

By making the game very similar to Bingo, Tara was able to complete the project quickly. She had great fun learning the vocabulary words at the same time. In the process her younger brother and sister learned all the words, too!

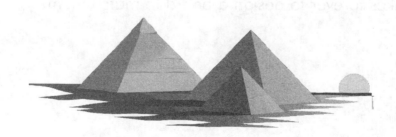

HOMEMADE GAME #4
A is for Amsterdam

Materials
- Large map posted where everyone can see it
- Paper and pencil for each player
- Timer (optional)

Do you remember the old parlor game called "Categories"? These "rules" are flexible. Structure them based on the age and ability of the players. Play in teams or individually. Different ages can compete together by handicapping the older ones with less time to complete their grid.

Directions
1. Pick a time limit. (Between 2 and 5 minutes works well.)
2. Each player writes as many names of places or physical features that begin with the letter "A" as he can see on the map. (Use a different letter each time you play.)
3. When time is up, count one point per word found.
4. If you'd like to challenge older students, you might have them cross out any word(s) that someone else has also found.

Variation
Within a given time limit, each player finds on the map and lists every name of physical and political features that begin with the letter "A."
For example: Amsterdam, Amazon River, Alps, etc.

Or pick a different letter each time and work in teams. Race against the clock to see how many names your team can find in a 5 or 10 minute block.

A IS FOR AMSTERDAM STUDENT ACTIVITY SHEET

NAME:_____

DATE: _____

DIRECTIONS

Using a world map and a timer, find as many rivers beginning with A, B, C, D, and E, then lakes and so on, as you can.

	RIVER	LAKE/SEA	CITY	COUNTRY	ISLAND/ATOLL
A					
B					
C					
D					
E					

Now it is your turn. Using the blank chart above, make up your own rules!

HOMEMADE GAME #5
Who Am I?

Materials
- ◆ Paper
- ◆ Pencils
- ◆ Atlas

Directions

Each player prepares a written description of a country that he chooses. One player reads his description, being careful not to mention the name of the country. The player who first identifies correctly the country described is the next to read his description. He calls on someone else to identify the country described. Cities, rivers, or important persons could also be used.

For example, "An animal that lives in this country has a unique "pocketbook" in which it holds its babies."

HOMEMADE GAME #6
Geography Bowl

■■

Materials

- A geography reference book or almanac.
- Little prizes or something with which to keep score. (Optional -- at our house we sometimes use mini-marshmallows or chocolate chips!)

Directions

1. Gather around the table. This is great for dinnertime when dad can play too!

2. Moderator looks at the reference material and formulates a question based on the ability of the player being asked. (Optional -- you may have students work in teams or they may have an open atlas or map in front of them.)

3. If player is correct he/she can either go again, win a prize, or get a point. (This is a very flexible game!)

Note

This makes great practice for the National Geography Bee. Or have your own version of the bee within your family. Winner gets out of the dishes that night??

Chapter 2
Homemade Books

Why Homemade Books?

What do homemade books have to do with geography? Making books can be a wonderful hands-on way to solidify a child's knowledge in any subject. The process is interesting and much is learned in the making of the book and the end result is a book the kids love to read over and over again -- thereby reinforcing the information taught in the book. In this chapter are examples, ideas, and resources to inspire you to include the making of books in your home.

This project can be used to introduce a topic, for assessment of what they've learned, as a fun project in the middle of their studies, or as an end-of-unit wrap-up. Similar to making games, the process of making the book requires them to learn the information at hand -- whether it is an overview of the subject or a detailed report of a specific topic. Design the project parameters to meet the needs of the students.

What are Homemade Books?

Kids' books can take on a variety of shapes and forms from simple manilla folders with handwritten pages stapled inside, to very elaborate, decorated books sewn together and covered with contact paper. Especially creative children will enjoy coming up with their own ideas for making books.

Types of Book Projects

ABC Books

Why an ABC book? That sounds like it's for preschoolers! Actually, making an ABC book is good for all ages; even much older students can benefit from this project. The idea is to have one page for each letter in the alphabet. On each page is written a word starting with the appropriate letter and pertaining to the study at hand. For example, while studying Rome one might use "Gladiator" for "G" and "Apostle Paul" for "A." After selecting the word, write in its definition or perhaps use it in a sentence. Then the student draws a picture to represent the word. Choose both important words for them to know and words that will be fun for them to depict. Although the word "citizen" is useful to know in the context of early Rome, "chariot races" would be easier to define and draw. Allow them lots of room to be creative here and to have some say in the words chosen.

Shape Books

Draw the shape of something indicative to your study, for example a volcano shape; photocopy as many pages of the shape as you need and then cut out the shape. Write one fact you've learned on each of the pages and then assemble into a book. The front cover could be done in cardstock for durability. The front and back covers can be illustrated and written on in the same way as your children's favorite books. It's especially appealing to add an "About the Author" section with picture and personal facts on the back of the book. Don't forget to date these family treasures!

Bound Books

Book projects can be bound in a number of different ways: from stapling them into a manilla folder, to sewing them together with dental floss, to glueing the pages onto sturdy fabric-covered cardboard, to three-ring-binders. A simple way to bind your project is to take it to your local copy shop. There you have choices like heat binding or spiral binding. Make sure you take your young authors with you to see their book get turned into a "finished" project!

Science and Geography: Two for the Price of One!

Field Guides

See pages 64 and 65 to learn more about making this type of book. The reproducible pages are designed for you to simply photocopy and bind. Science and geography are a terrific twosome!

Justin Roams the Rivers

Pick a natural resource found in your area to study, recording what is learned in a notebook. For example, do you have rivers or streams nearby? Use maps to identify rivers found in your area. Where do they come from and where do they go? In what way do they impact the environment? In what way has man impacted them? These are natural geographic questions. When they are finished with the research, illustrate it and bind it into a book.

Exploding Volcanoes!

Pop-up books are great fun to make and can illustrate concepts in a way more difficult in typical flat books. *Super Pop-Ups* and *More Super Pop-Ups* by Joan Irvine have great suggestions and directions for these types of books, including a pop-up volcano.

Once Upon a Time

Not every book dealing with geography needs to be non-fiction! Much can be learned by simply setting a story in another place. The student will then need to learn something about that places, climate, culture, physical features, etc. in order for her characters to really live there.

Happily Ever After

Don't forget to take these books off the bookshelf to share with friends and family and to read occasionally as part of your reading routine. Not only does that reinforce the information contained in the book, it also encourages your student to write some more!

On the next page are directions for a durable and attractive book about early America. The same idea can be used to do a book about any country or time period you're studying.

The Early American Book

Materials

- Books, atlases, and other reference material
- Note paper
- Art supplies for illustrations
- Clean notebook paper for the final copy
- Three-pronged folder or other binder

Directions

1. Define the goal of this book. Will it be a general description of what your student has learned about early America? Or will it have a narrower focus like "Life in a Colonial Town"?

2. Decide on the style of the book: Shape, ABC, other.

3. Make a simple outline/rough draft. (A simple sentence or two per page is acceptable.)

4. Copy the final work onto clean notebook paper.

5. Illustrate.

6. Design cover page with title, author, copyright symbol, date, even acknowledgments.

7. Design front cover with title and author's name.

8. Design back cover with "About the Author" and perhaps a photograph of the student.

9. Three-ring hole punch all pages to fit into folder or bind at the copy shop.

10. Voila -- you have a book!

Note

Circulate this book! Share it with friends and family, read it aloud to siblings, use it as a reference! If the project was an enjoyable experience it will encourage your young author to write more.

Resources for Homemade Books

Big Book of Books and Activities by Dinah Zike
This book contains the most incredible bookmaking ideas! A wealth of suggestions with reproducible pages and complete directions. Appropriate for pre-school through junior high school. Very easy to follow directions. Ideal for all subject areas.

Creating Books with Children by Valerie Bendt
Your child will create a lifetime keepsake following the directions in this book for an elaborate homemade book. Comes complete with directions, lessons, samples, diagrams, and photographs.

Super Pop-Ups and *More Super Pop-Ups* by Joan Irvine
Although the directions in this book are intended to make one page greeting card-type projects, the ideas are neat and fun to do. One could even put several pop-up cards together and call it a pop-up book!

Dover Publications

Dover coloring books are useful resources. These inexpensive books offer detailed pictures and little nuggets of information on a wide variety of topics. Studying the states? Dover publishes books on state birds and one on state flowers. Civil War, Ancient Greece, Costumes, Transportation, etc. are just a couple of the huge variety of coloring books available. These are handy for cutting out pictures to use in illustrating homemade books or to help in the design of front and back covers. Good for children who don't like to draw as well as a great idea book for children that do! Widely available. For a complete catalog write:

Dover Publications, Inc.
31 East 2nd Street
Mineola, NY 11501

Chapter 3
My Country Notebook

When learning about new countries, research and map work is valuable. Equally valuable however, is getting to know the people and culture of the country. Get a taste of another land without leaving your hometown! By completing a "My Country Notebook" kids will discover the heartbeat of the country.

Photocopy as many "My Country Notebooks" as you need for your students. The cover page may be illustrated or pictures and postcards may be pasted on it. Students will need help in looking up information and filling in the pages. This is a good time to gently introduce some research/library skills to them. Dictation is allowed -- children who do not have strong writing skills may benefit from dictating the information to the teacher who then faithfully records the words. Not every line needs to be filled in!! For younger children an entire page or two could be dropped. Take the needs and abilities of students into consideration.

Find the best resources. Use the library and friends. Dig up music, art, videos, magazines, costumes, etc. Cook dishes together. Make a craft. Build a typical house. Draw a map. Using a variety of activities will make this country come alive in a way that book learning just cannot do. This project makes a great lead-in to hosting a "Passport Luncheon" as described on page 37.

This is certainly one of those activities that will be as simple or complex as you prefer.

My Country Notebook

MY COUNTRY IS:_____

NAME: _____ **DATE:** _____

What continent is your country on?

Who are its neighbors?

What body or bodies of water is it near or in?

What's its climate?

What are some of its physical features?

What is its capital?

What are the native (indigenous) people called?

What did you learn about them?

Plants and animals that are native to this country include:

Learn about their art and show or tell what you've learned.

What kinds of houses do people live in?

Listen to their music. What is it like?

What languages are spoken there?

I learned these words:

A country is more than a place on a map. Here are some of the things I learned about the culture of this country:

What religion is most common?

Are Christians persecuted for their beliefs?

What form of government does this country have?

What does their flag look like?

Show and tell what you learned about their money:

Here's a typical breakfast, lunch, and dinner for a student like me:

This is what I learned about their clothing:

Vocabulary words I learned studying this country:

Activities and projects I did:

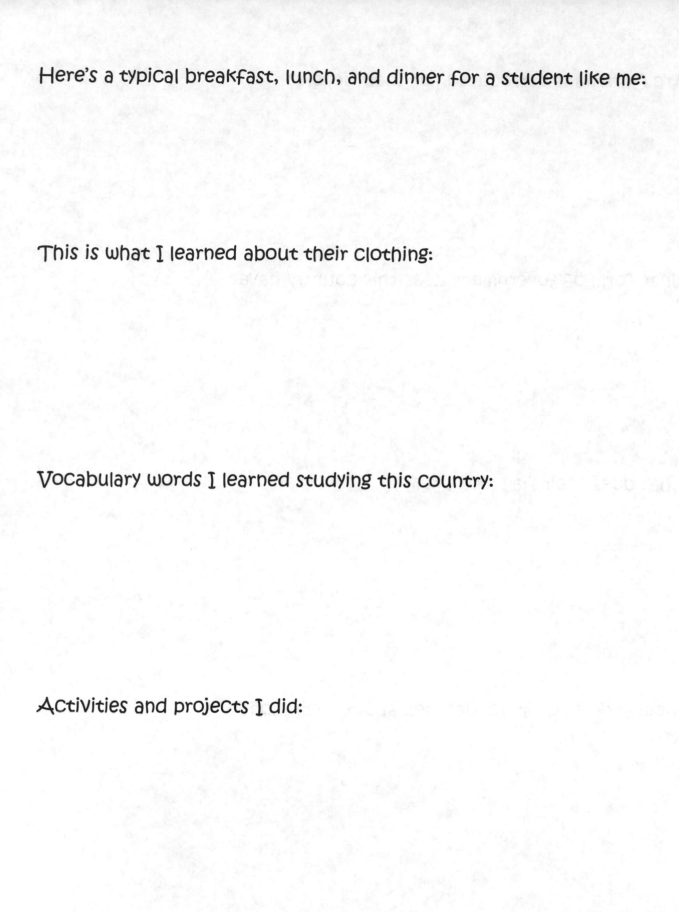

People I spoke with or places I visited:

Materials and references I used in compiling this notebook:

Christmas in _____

Do people have the freedom to celebrate Christ's birth at home and in school?

Special customs, stories, songs, and food they have at Christmas include:

This is how they say "Merry Christmas" in their language:

Their Christmas is similar to mine because:

Their Christmas is different from mine because:

Chapter 4
Passport Fair or Around the World Night

A Passport Fair is a terrific way to end a study of a place or time period. It can be as simple as preparing a few foods from that place or era and serving it to your family or as elaborate as an entire homeschool group sharing what they've learned. Our homeschool group has done this for a number of years now using the gym in our church. This is also fun to do with just a few families in your own home. Either way, it is a great finale to your study! Consider holding it at night or on a weekend so that more dads and other family members may attend.

What is Needed

Families -- each chooses a state, region, or country they'd like to learn about.
Location -- arrange a space large enough to accommodate your group.
Passport books for each student attending. Photocopy the example passport on page 38 to use with your group.

Directions

1. Each family will setup and man a booth displaying the results of their study. For example, their booth might include any or all of the following:

   — postcards   — posters
   — artwork   — music
   — crafts   — reports
   — brochures   — costumes
   — dioramas   — souvenirs
   — representative snacks — stamps
   — currency

2. Each booth will have a map displayed, either bought or homemade.

3. Each family provides:

   A. Stamps or stickers representative of their chosen area to place in each attendee's passport.
   B. "Fact Sheets" about their country for each participant.
   C. A labeled main dish, side dish, dessert, or snacks using recipes from the chosen country.

4. Allow enough time at the luncheon for families to visit booths, see displays, get passports stamped, and read fact sheets.

The Secretary of State of the United States of America hereby request all whom it may concern to permit the citizen/national of the United States named herein to pass without delay or hindrance and in case of need to give all lawful aid and protection.

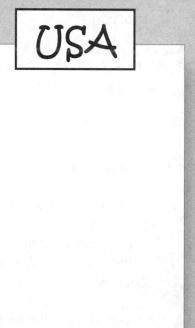

USA

PLACE PHOTO HERE

SIGNATURE OF BEARER

NOT VALID UNTIL SIGNED

Chapter 5
Joseph's Journey

Joseph's Journey is an adventure through the life of Joseph that gives us an opportunity for some "hands-on" geography.

Materials
- NIV Bible
- Paper and color pencils or markers
- Topographical map of Israel, Jordan, and Egypt (optional)

Map locations in Genesis specified by verse

Canaan-37:1	Dothan-37:17	Egypt-37:25, et al
Gilead-37:25	Shechem-37:12	Valley of Hebron-37:14

Other major geographical features

Dead Sea	Gulf of Aqaba	Heliopolis (On)
Gulf of Suez	Jordan River	Mediterranean Sea
Nile River	Red Sea	Sea of Galilee
Sinai Desert		

Bible references
Genesis 16, 25, 37
Judges 8

Overview
Study the story of Joseph, his being sold into slavery, life in Egypt, appointment by Pharaoh, and eventual reunion with his family. By tracing his travels, the student will identify on the map the location of each city and area. By reviewing a physical topography map, your student can also identify important features such as mountains, rivers, valleys, deserts, plains, etc.

This Bible study centers on Genesis 37, from the time Joseph was 17 until he was sold to Potiphar. Interwoven in the study are short and simple map activities. The student map and answer map are at the end of the study, along with a teacher answer key. By the end of this short study, students will have a strong grasp of the geography of this area.

Bible studies become deeper and richer by looking more closely at the geography. Familiar stories take on new life as the geography is unveiled. Use this study as an example for future Bible studies.

Questions

1. In what land did Joseph and his family live?
    ACTIVITY: Shade the area on your map in green to show the land in which Joseph and his family lived. (Joseph's family lived in the territory west of the areas known as the Sea of Galilee, the River Jordan, and the Dead Sea.)

2. What animals were raised in this area?

3. Why did Jacob love Joseph more than his other sons?

4. How did he show his love?

5. How did Joseph's brothers react?

6. What was Joseph's first dream?

7. What was Joseph's second dream?

8. What did his father understand this dream to mean?

9. In Genesis 37:12, where did Joseph's brothers take their flocks to graze?
 ACTIVITY: On your map, locate and label this city. This city is west of the River Jordan, mid-way between the Sea of Galilee and the Dead Sea.

10. According to Genesis 37:14, from where did Joseph leave to go to his brothers?
 ACTIVITY: On your map locate and label this area. This city is about 15 miles west of the mid-point of the Dead Sea.

11. When Joseph arrived in Shechem, where was he told he might find his brothers?
 ACTIVITY: On your map locate and label this area. This city is about 20 miles north of Shechem.

12. Is Dothan cool, green and fertile, or dry and sandy?
 ACTIVITY: Color the area around Dothan a sandy color.

13. What is a cistern?

14. Why would there be a cistern in the desert?

15. Why did Joseph's brothers plot to kill him?

16. Who secretly planned to save him?

17. Use a dictionary to define "caravan."

18. Who were the Ismaelites?

ACTIVITY: On your map, label the area known as Midian and shade it in yellow. Midian is an area occupying the eastern shore of the Gulf of Aqaba.

19. Where was Gilead?

ACTIVITY: On your map, locate and label this area. Gilead is the area east of the River Jordan extending from north of the Dead Sea to south of the Sea of Galilee.

20. Where were the Ishmaelites heading?

ACTIVITY: On your map, locate and label this country and shade it in blue. This country occupies the lands bordering the Nile River and Delta.

21. Why were the Ishmaelites going there?

22. What business transactions did Joseph's brothers make with the Ishmaelites/Midians?

23. What was Reuben's reaction when he learned what his brothers had done to Joseph?

24. How did Joseph's brothers try to cover up their treacherous deed?

25. What did Jacob do when he saw the red robe?

26. Where did the Ishmaelites/Midians take Joseph?

27. Who bought him?

ACTIVITY:

a. In black, trace the route of Joseph from the Valley of Hebron to Shechem, Dothan and then to Egypt.

b. In red, trace the route of the Ishmaelites from their homeland in Midian, up to Gilead, across the River Jordan, to Dothan, along the coast to the Egyptian city of Heliopolis. (On.)

Answer Sheet (according to NIV references)

1. In what land did Joseph and his family live?
   Canaan (Genesis 37:1)

2. What animals were raised in this area?
   Flocks of animals including sheep and goats. (Genesis 37:2, 31)

3. Why did Jacob love Joseph more than his other sons?
   Because he had been born to him in his old age. (Genesis 37:3)

4. How did he show his love?
   He gave him a special richly ornamented robe. (Genesis 37:3)

5. How did Joseph's brothers react?
   They hated him and could not speak a kind word to him. (Genesis 37:4)

6. What was Joseph's first dream?
   The binding of sheaves of grain (see full account in Genesis 37:5-7)

7. What was Joseph's second dream?
   Sun, moon, and seven stars (see full account in Genesis 37:9)

8. What did his father understand this dream to mean?
   Joseph's father, mother, and brothers would come and bow down to the ground before Joseph. (Genesis 37:10)

9. In Genesis 37:12, where did Joseph's brothers take their flocks to graze?
   Near Shechem. (Genesis 37:12)

10. According to Genesis 37:14, from where did Joseph leave to go to his brothers?
    The Valley of Hebron. (Genesis 37:14)

11. When Joseph arrived in Shechem, where was he told he might find his brothers?
    Dothan, about 20 miles north of Shechem. (Genesis 37:17)

12. Is Dothan cool, green and fertile, or dry and sandy?
    Dry and sandy (a desert). (Genesis 37:22)

13. What is a cistern?
    A reservoir or tank for storing water or other liquid.

14. Why would there be a cistern in the desert?
    To hold and store scarce and precious water.

15. Why did Joseph's brothers plot to kill him?
    They hated him because he was their father's favorite. (Genesis 37:3-4)

16. Who secretly planned to save him?
    His brother Reuben. (Genesis 37:22)

17. Use a dictionary to define "caravan."
    A group of travelers, as merchants or pilgrims, banded together for safety in journeying through deserts, hostile territory, etc.

18. Who were the Ismaelites?
    Ishmaelite and Midianite merchants: both of these groups of desert-dwellers were descended from Abraham. The names are interchangeable. (From *Eerdmans Handbook to the Bible*, 1992, page 146.) Also see Genesis 37:28 & 36, Genesis 16:15, Genesis 25:2 and 18, Judges 8:24. (Location taken from *The Route of the Exodus*, 1986, The Moody Bible Institute of Chicago.)

19. Where was Gilead?
    Gilead is an area east of the River Jordan extending from north of the Dead Sea to south of the Sea of Galilee. (From *Palestine: Political Regions*, 1986, The Moody Bible Institute of Chicago.)

20. Where were the Ishmaelites heading?
    Egypt. (Genesis 37:25)

21. Why were the Ishmaelites going there?
    They planned to sell or trade their load of spices, balm, and myrrh. (Genesis 37:25)

22. What business transactions did Joseph's brothers make with the Ishmaelites/Midians?
    They sold Joseph to the merchants for 20 shekels of silver. (Genesis 37:28)

23. What was Reuben's reaction when he learned what his brothers had done to Joseph?
    He tore his clothes, went back to his brothers and said, "The boy isn't there! Where can I turn now?" (Genesis 37:29)

24. How did Joseph's brothers try to cover up their treacherous deed?
    They took Joseph's robe, slaughtered a goat and dipped the robe in blood. They presented the robe to Jacob who recognized it as Joseph's. Jacob thought that some ferocious animal had devoured Joseph and that Joseph had surely been torn to pieces. (Genesis 37:31-33)

25. What did Jacob do when he saw the red robe?
    Jacob tore his clothes, put on sackcloth and mourned for his son many days. (Genesis 37:34)

26. Where did the Ishmaelites/Midians take Joseph?
    Egypt. (Genesis 37:25)

27. Who bought him?
    Potiphar, one of Pharaoh's officials, the captain of the guard. (Genesis 37:36)

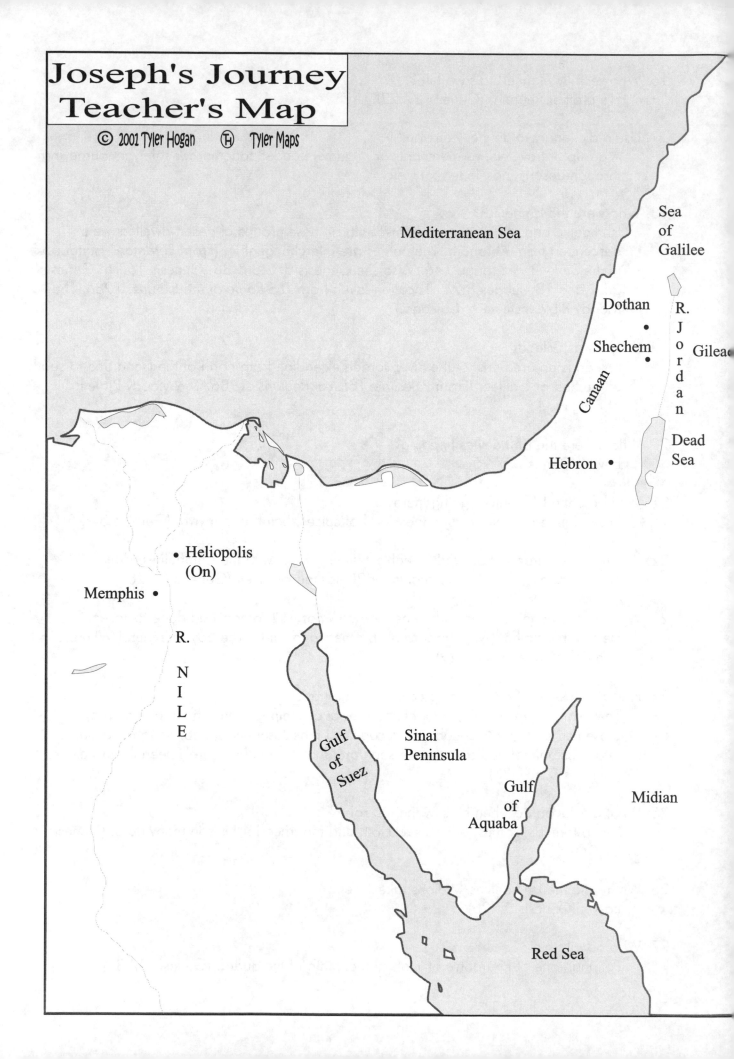

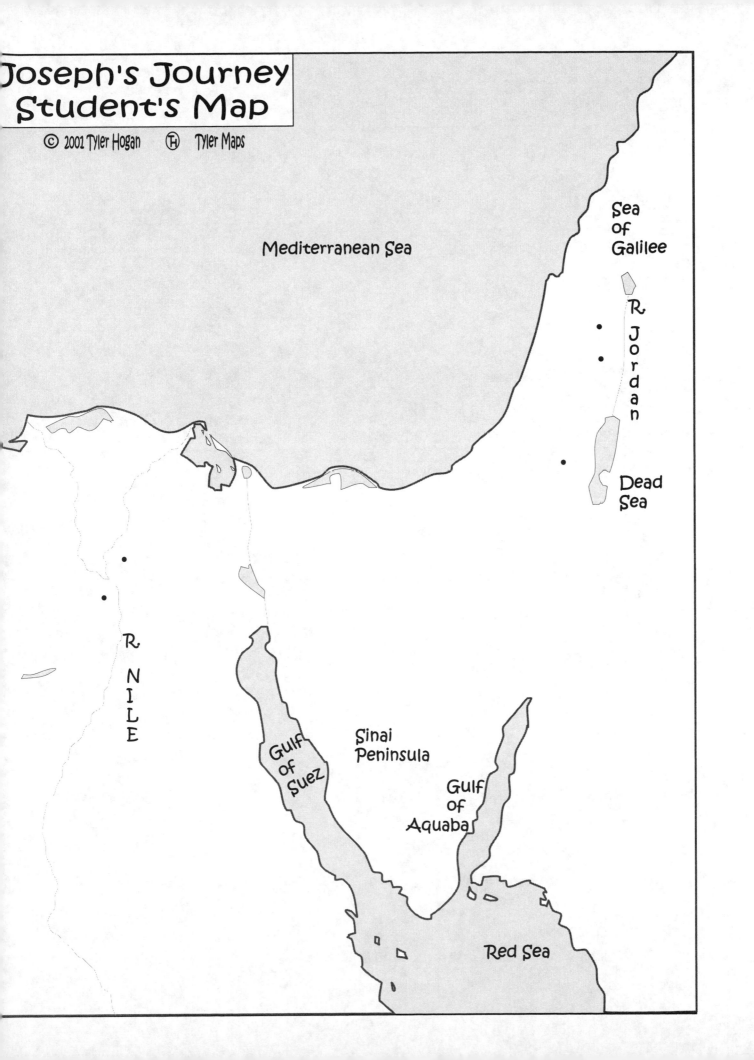

Joseph's Journey Student's Map

© 2001 Tyler Hogan   Ⓣ   Tyler Maps

Mediterranean Sea

Sea of Galilee

R Jordan

Dead Sea

R NILE

Gulf of Suez

Sinai Peninsula

Gulf of Aquaba

Red Sea

Chapter 6
Missionary Geography

"He (Jesus) said to them: It is not for you to know the times or dates the Father has set by His own authority. But you will receive power when the Holy Spirit comes on you; and you will be my witnesses in Jerusalem, and in all Judea and Samaria, and to the ends of the earth." Acts 1:7-8 (NIV)

"As for me, far be it from me that I should sing against the Lord by failing to pray for you." 1 Samuel 12:23 (NIV)

"And pray in the Spirit on all occasions with all kinds of prayers and requests. With this in mind, be alert and always keep on praying for all the saints." Ephesians 6:18 (NIV)

We are called to pray for one another. We pray with our children about concerns and praises within our family, church and community. Do we remember to pray with them about people internationally? One way people do this is by praying for specific missions and missionaries as well as through offerings and correspondence.

Often missionary families have children, either in boarding school or with them on the mission field. Perhaps your family can begin to write to them regularly. Robin Stewart and her husband, parents of four and for many years missionaries stationed in France, shared this: "Something as simple as a postcard with greetings and a favorite memory verse means a lot to the children. Just realize that for various reasons, they cannot always return your note. Think of it as a ministry of encouragement."

The resources and activities on the next few pages will give you some ideas on how to incorporate geography into missionary support and prayer. Use these ideas as a jumping off point in planning your lessons. Praise God for the diversity of our world and for His people who have dedicated their lives to the sharing of the gospel to the ends of the earth!

Missionary Geography Ideas

♦ Study the life of a missionary. Use biographies. Study the geography of his or her mission field. Act out a dramatic scene. Draw or paint a picture of their mission world. YWAM publishes terrific books on missionaries for the 8-12 crowd that make great read-alouds.

♦ Learn more about your church's or your denomination's missionaries. Where do they serve? What is it like being a missionary in this day and time?

♦ Choose a country, continent, or people group. Pray for the unsaved people there. Pray for serving missionaries. Use *You Can Change the World* volumes 1 or 2 to discover prayer requests and much more.

♦ Write missionaries and/or their children. Earn money to send them special gifts. They especially appreciate children's Christian literature, music, and magazines. Save your old "Clubhouse" magazines to mail in a batch, or enter a gift subscription in their name.

- Make a missionary map. Attach pictures of missionaries you are studying to the appropriate countries.

- Find out what time it is in your chosen country. If you pray for your missionaries at lunchtime, what time is it where they are? Should you be praying that they wake up refreshed or for a good night's rest? This is a wonderful method to make time zones meaningful!

- Make a missionary or country "Prayer-a-Day Calendar." Have students draw a monthly calendar (or print a blank one off of your computer.) Pick a specific prayer request for each day or week. Check it off each day as you pray for them.

- Borrow or purchase a Bible in another language. Copy favorite scripture and post it. Why do we need Bibles in other languages? How do people go about translating the Bible? What languages was the Bible originally written in? Read a biography of Wycliff or other Bible translators.

- Learn a Christian song in another language. Try your library or church for tapes of songs and scripture in foreign languages. What would it be like to be a missionary's child and go to a land where you didn't speak the language?

- Try and attend missionary meetings when they come back on leave. Think ahead of time about the questions you would like answered. Ask them for prayer requests.

Missions Relief Map

Materials
* Salt map dough (see recipe on next page)
* Piece of smooth wood, cookie tray, or other sturdy surface
* Tempera paints
* Clay dough
* Various toys and household scraps
* Topographical map of country being studied
* Reference books

Directions
1. Make salt dough based on recipe on next page.

2. Draw map outline onto wood, or tape an enlarged copy of the map directly onto the flat surface you're using.

3. Spoon on dough and spread it out. Build up for mountains, carve out lakes, rivers, valleys, etc.

4. Let dry thoroughly then paint.

5. While it is drying, begin to make a village on or next to the map.

6. Use clay dough for rocks, cooking pots, housing, etc.

7. Use clothes pins or chenille wires to form people. Learn about native dress and get creative with your little people!

8. Build the missionary compound out of appropriate materials. (Thatched huts or bricks?)

9. Use aluminum foil for water, twigs and weeds for trees and bushes. Spread on glue and pour on sand where appropriate.

This is a great group project to do over several bad-weather days. (Although moisture in the air will slow down the salt dough drying.) While the map is drying students can be learning about the country and people from your resource and reference books. Encourage authenticity but be flexible! Some things are just hard to duplicate. While they are working, read aloud to them out of first-rate exciting books about the land of a person who lived there. Allowed some freedom, kids will take off on this project. Don't forget to take pictures of the finished product!

Missions Relief Map (continued)

Encourage your students to write about what they learned and attach it to their map/diorama. After the masterpiece is done, see if you can display it in your church or library.

****

Salt Dough Recipe

Salt dough maps are easy, inexpensive, and unbeatable for tactile learners! Making a salt dough map at the beginning of your history studies is a sure-fire method for students to truly learn the "lay of the land." History is more meaningful when they have a solid grasp of the "where" of it.

Materials for Salt Dough
- 2 cups flour
- 1 cup salt
- Water -- enough to make dough sticky but workable

Materials for Map
- Reference atlases
- Salt dough
- Heavy piece of cardboard
- Copy of an outline map (optional, but very handy!)
- Food coloring or poster paints (optional)

Directions
1. Glue outline map to cardboard leaving at least one inch around the border for ease in carrying. If you'd like to have a key, leave a blank space for it.

2. Mix dough ingredients.

3. Optional: separate dough and then color it according to physical features i.e., blue for water, green for land, brown for desert, etc.

4. Using a physical reference map in an atlas, place dough on map by color, according to physical features. Build up mountain ranges; make valleys and lakes, etc.

5. Optional -- when dry, paint with poster paints.

6. Make a key and attach to the border of the map.

Tip
Salt dough maps take much longer to dry on wet or muggy days. After map dries, take a picture of it. Salt dough maps don't "save" well, but pictures do!

Missionary Resources

Wycliffe Bible Translators
P.O. Box 628200
Orlando, FL 32862-2000
800.992.5433 or
407.852.3600
www.wycliffe.org

ABS Interactive
American Bible Society
1865 Broadway
New York, NY 10023
800.32.BIBLE
www.americanbible.org

Adopt-A-People Clearinghouse
P.O. Box 63600
Colorado Springs, CO 80962-3600
719.574.7001
www.aapc.net
mail@aapc.net
Adopt-A-People publish a series of country profiles in the size and format of passports, providing information more detailed than that in *You Can Change the World*. Write for available countries and prices.

YWAM Publishing
Youth With a Mission (YWAM) is an international missionary organization of Christians from many denominations dedicated to presenting Jesus Christ to this generation. Their catalog is filled with terrific mission-minded books for youth and adults. Check out their series "Christian Heroes: Then and Now," biographies of great missionaries written for youth. They carry the excellent children's resources *You Can Change the World* Volumes I & II. These A-Z guides to countries and people groups that need to hear the gospel include stories, charts, maps, facts, color illustrations, and prayer ideas. Highly recommended -- go to the "bookstore" link!
www.ywam.org

Voice of the Martyrs
This organization puts a global perspective on the persecution of God's children. Check out their great web site, including a section for kids. Sign up on-line for their free (and worthwhile) newsletter, The Link.
www.persecution.com

Chapter 7
Genealogy Geography

Where do you come from? Do your children know where their relatives were born and raised? The following activity teaches geography in a very personal way. By bringing family, stories, and customs into the picture, children get excited about history and geography. Uncle Dave is moving to Oman? Where is that?!

By hearing from, reading about, and talking with relatives who are from outside your hometown area, you're exposing your children to tales that make geography and history come alive. This activity is a great kick-off. Start with this, then use your imagination to create a custom-made genealogy geography project for your family.

You'll have to do some detective work ahead of time in order to have the necessary information on hand to begin the project. Older students will enjoy helping to gather facts and anecdotes but younger students may lose interest before the hands-on part begins.

Materials Needed for Each Option
- Collection of anecdotes from immediate family members. Include stories from as far back as possible. These don't have to be long or "important" stories.
- Pictures of as many relatives as possible.
- Pictures of common items from the time period being discussed. (This is the type of telephone Grandma would have used, etc.)
- Atlas

Option #1 3-D Genealogy Map
Additional Materials
- Easy-to-read map, tacked down to a piece of foam board.
- Little people to represent family members
- Small animals, toys, houses, etc.
- Index cards cut in thirds & markers
- Double-sided tape

Directions
1. Put the foam-backed map on a card table where it can remain undisturbed for the length of this project.

2. After reading or listening to stories about a relative, find their home on the map or atlas.

3. Then choose a figure to represent that person and place it on the map; use tape for stability.

4. Write a brief synopsis of the story on an index card and attach it to the map near the corresponding person.

Option #2 Homemade Genealogy Notebook
Additional Materials
- Three-ring-binder and notebook paper
- Art supplies

Directions
1. Read stories and talk about relatives.

2. Record information you've learned about each person on their own page.

3. Student illustrates their page.

4. After many relatives are discussed put the pages together in chronological order.

5. Design a cover for the book.

Option # 3 Timeline Genealogy
Additional Materials
- Paper or poster board
- Art supplies
- Magazines to cut out pictures to represent people and events on timeline.

Directions*
Make a timeline with the people involved; include dates familiar to the student. (Their own birthday, parents' birthdays, history dates they have learned, etc.) *See chapter on *Timelines* for more information.

Extensions
- ❑ Learn about the country or regions from which relatives descended.
- ❑ Cook food significant to those countries or regions of the USA.
- ❑ Cook a dish significant to your childhood: the special birthday cake or Christmas dish and explain why it is important to you.
- ❑ Compile a cookbook of favorite family recipes from both sides of your children's family tree. Add notes, photographs where available. This could become an heirloom book!
- ❑ Draw a large family tree with room to write in names on the individual leaves. Add to it as you complete the other projects.
- ❑ Place stickers on a large world wall map to represent where each person that you learn about comes from.
- ❑ Ask relatives from out of town to send postcards from their hometown.

Christmas Around the World

An appealing and informative study of geography can be wrapped around a unit on Christmas. What a great way to prepare for the celebration of the birthday of our Lord -- learning about His people here on earth and how they celebrate His birth.

Materials
- Bible
- World maps
- World atlas
- Encyclopedia
- References -- libraries usually have many books on celebrating Christmas around the world
- Notebook

Directions
Read the Christmas story. Find the places mentioned in the Bible account on your world map or in an atlas. Talk about the weather and terrain there. Was it hot or cold? Lush jungle, forest, desert, other?

From there discuss how Christmas came to be celebrated differently in different parts of the world. Look at some of the favorite American traditions and see how these differ from traditions elsewhere. Here are a few to get you started:

Tradition	Country	Description
Recipes	Czechoslovakia	Moravian Christmas Cookies
	Russia	Russian Walnuts
	Asia	Peanut Taffy
	France	Bûche de Noël
Ornaments	China & Japan	Origami
	Russia	The same Russian Walnuts
Caroling	Poland	Dressed as animals of the manger
	Greece	with lots of homemade instruments
Mangers	Latin America	"Creches" -- elaborate, large displays
Gift Wrapping	Sweden	Layers and layers of wrapping
Gingerbread Houses	Denmark	Popular custom, very elaborate
Going Mumming	Russia	Popular in Russia and other European countries -- Mummers dress up in colorful garments and visit and amuse their neighbors

Christmas Around the World (continued)

Secret Friends	Brazil	Give gifts to friends anonymously
Camel Rides	Australia	Of course!
Star Lanterns	Philippines	Called "Parols" -- very important and popular
Christmas Letters	Italy	Written to the parents

As you learn about customs around the world you'll learn about the people and cultures of many different places.

This would be a good time to pull out a prayer guide to use in praying for countries where Christians are persecuted or struggling. A favorite is *You Can Change the World*, now in two volumes. Here we learned that Christianity has been so removed from the culture in Uruguay that Christmas Day is now called Family Day and it is illegal to talk about religion in school or at the university. What a sobering reminder that we need to pray for and guard our religious freedom here in America, as well as pray for those in other countries.

A map could be colored in -- countries where Christ is honored at Christmas and countries where Christmas is not openly celebrated. How would we color in America?

Chapter 8
Nature and Geography

Birds and Geography

The migration and habitat of birds is as much geography as it is science. The science of studying birds is called Ornithology. Isn't it amazing how many different kinds of birds God made? From the large, strange-looking ostrich, to the beautiful parrot, and incredibly quick hummingbird, God has given us a tremendous variety of birds to watch and learn about.

City folks, suburban kids, and desert dwellers can all attract different kinds of birds. The first step? Go to the library and get books on birds common to your area. Find out what and where they like to eat. Then purchase seed or food and place it in a likely spot. One gentleman in an office building downtown faithfully puts seeds on his windowsill everyday. He attracts morning doves, chickadees and other species.

Watch! If birds haven't been frequenting your home, be patient. It may take a week or two but, if there is food, water, and some type of shelter, they will come. Once you have birds visiting, it is exciting to learn to identify them, tell if they're male or female, grown or juvenile, and to recognize their habits and songs.

All serious "birders" keep a bird log in which they note: kinds of birds they would have seen, where they spotted them, the weather, etc. It's satisfying to keep a simple list of each different bird spotted.

> *Look at the birds of the air; they do not sow or reap or store away in barns, and yet your heavenly Father feeds them. Are you not much more valuable than they? Matthew 6:26*

Other Activities
- ❏ Make a bird field guide using photographs or drawings of favorite birds.
- ❏ Make your own bird food, using recipes from bird books.
- ❏ Create a bird board game or card game.
- ❏ Borrow a bird call recording from your library. Learn a bird whistle.
- ❏ Build a feeder or nest box.
- ❏ Visit a local wildlife area, park or pet store to learn more about birds.

Words to Know:
Bird species: a group of closely related birds, that can breed and have offspring.
Bird genus: closely related species are grouped into a genus.
Habitat: where an animal lives; the particular environment it needs to survive.
Range: the area over which a species of bird is found.

Complete the two charts on the following pages.

Activity 1
Migration

Discover what birds are common to your area.

Chart their route on a large wall map or make your own migratory maps.

Answer these questions:

- ❑ Why do these birds live where they do?
- ❑ Why do they migrate?
- ❑ Where do they migrate to?
- ❑ What foods do they eat during different seasons? How does that affect where they live?

	Observation #1	Observation #2	Observation #3	Observation #4
BIRD NAME	Purple Martin			
MIGRATES FROM	Brazil			
LIVES HERE DURING	Spring and Summer			
RETURNS TO	Brazil			

Activity 2
Bird Habitat

Pick several birds that live in your area. Read about them. What can you do to attract them to your yard? The first one is filled in for you.

	Observation #1	Observation #2	Observation #3	Observation #4
BIRD NAME	Ruby-throated hummingbird			
FAVORITE FOODS	Nectar, insects, sap, sugar water, and bright red flowers			
HABITAT	Mixed woodlands			
NESTING	Nest is often built by small bodies of water			

Do-It-Yourself Field Guides

This is a rewarding project that any nature lover will enjoy. What would you like to study? Flowers, trees, butterflies, rocks, frogs? The possibilities are huge. Where might you find your specimens?

Pick a likely habitat to explore. (Make sure you have permission to walk around in this place and only collect specimens with permission.) Even if collections are possible, one can always make observations, record notes, photograph and make drawings.

Materials
- Notebook
- Pen/color pencils
- Appropriate container for specimens
- Gloves or net if collecting live specimens
- Optional: camera

Directions
Visit your chosen habitat. Look around. Does this appear to be a likely place to find your specimens? If so, open your notebook and record the following information:

- ☐ Name or location of place
- ☐ Type of habitat
- ☐ Date
- ☐ Time
- ☐ Weather
- ☐ Comments

As you collect live specimens, note in your book what it was doing, sounds it was making, and where it was found. (For example: This small black insect was under a rock, tunneling furiously into the ground.)

If you have a camera, take a picture of it in its habitat, or else draw a quick color sketch. Release insects after observation. When you're through collecting for the day, bring everything home. Spend time right away with a field guide or encyclopedia trying to identify specimens while your memory is fresh.

Do-It-Yourself Field Guides (continued)

Use one of the following pages to make copies for your own field guide. The first page is intended for critter-type specimens and the second page is for *flowers, rocks, shells, trees, **leaves. etc.

After you have filled in a page for each specimen and added your photographs or pictures, make a cover and display your own custom-made field guide!

*Pressed flowers: To press flowers, gather dry flowers, arrange them on a sheet of typing paper, lay another sheet on top of them. Stack several heavy books on top. Leave for 2-3 weeks. Paste into your field guide.

**Preserved leaves: Spread out your specimens on a hard surface. Pound the stems with a lightweight hammer. Inside, stir together 3 parts of hot tap water to 1 part glycerine (available from drug stores). Place the plant stems in the mixture. In about a week the stems will be pliable. Then take them out of the mixture, dry, and add to your field guide. (One method would be to paste them onto a page and then cover the page with contact paper.)

Extension

If you like an alternative to collecting specimens, a sky journal might be just the thing! Observe the sky every day at about the same time. Write down your observations:
- ☐ color of the sky
- ☐ types of clouds
- ☐ amount of coverage
- ☐ temperature
- ☐ wind speed
- ☐ wind direction

Use a Cloud Chart (see resources) or book about clouds to identify the clouds you observe. Carefully note the weather each day and make your weather forecast for the next day.

Draw and label the clouds for your own Cloud Field Guide.

Nature Field Guide
"Critter" Observations

Name _____

Date _____

HABITAT _____

_____

_____

COMMON NAME _____

_____

SPECIES _____

_____

SIZE _____

_____

COLORATION _____

_____

FEEDS ON _____

_____

_____

ACTION OBSERVED _____

_____

_____

_____

FIELD NOTES/SKETCHES _____

_____

_____

_____

Nature Field Guide
Plant Observations

Name _____

Date _____

HABITAT _____

_____

_____

_____

COMMON NAME _____ _____

_____

SPECIES _____

_____

SIZE _____

_____

COLORATION _____

_____

FIELD NOTES/SKETCHES _____

_____

_____

_____

_____

_____

_____

_____

_____

Passport to Your National Parks

We've had fun over the years having our own National Park Passport stamped (canceled) at each National Park we visit. The Passport book is under ten dollars and may be purchased at any National Park Visitor Center. It is filled with information and pictures about each of America's National Parks, divided by regions. The Passport Book is useful for planning trips and once stamped, serves as a souvenir for every National Park you visit.

To have your book stamped, take it to the Visitor Center and look for the simple rubber stamp with the name of the park and the date of your visit. Find the matching park in your Passport book and stamp (or to use real passport jargon: "cancel") it.

This book then serves as both an informational book and a memory book for all the parks you visit over your lifetime. The stamp cancellations are not available by mail -- only in person at each park. Don't panic if you arrive at a National Park and you've left home without your passport! Having done this several times ourselves we quickly figured out we could stamp a piece of paper and then tape it into our book when we arrived back home.

Additionally, each year the Park Service issues a sheet of color Passport Stamps. The set of ten stamps (one national and nine regional) is enclosed on one sticker sheet for under five dollars. Each sticker can then be peeled off and placed in the designated area in your Passport. You may purchase stamps (including those issued in previous years) by contacting the National Park Service.

America's National Parks
470 Maryland Drive Suite 2
Ft. Washington, PA 19034
877.Nat-Park
www.Nationalparkbooks.org

Junior Park Ranger Program

Many of the National Parks have a Junior Park Ranger Program. Ask at the ticket counter or visitor center when you arrive. To participate children will receive a free booklet with questions and activities related to that specific park. By paying attention to either the Ranger Tour or to the signs posted throughout the Visitor Center and park, they will fill out the age-appropriate pages and then return the booklet to the Visitor Center for a Park Ranger to check. A completed booklet earns students a Junior Park Ranger certificate and badge.

The activities in the booklet are divided into age groups:

☐   6 & under
☐   7-9
☐   10 & up.

Working on the booklet adds focus and motivation for students to pay close attention to the surroundings.

Note
You may run into evolutionary or politically correct doctrine at some parks.

Chapter 9
Language Arts and Geography

Literature and Geography

Great books are a great place to turn to learn more about geography! Simply mapping stories is certainly a fine activity but if you want to really dig into a book, try a complete unit study. Choose a book with a strong geographic theme, depth, and detail. The classics are usually good places to look. The following is an outline of a complete unit study using Around the World in Eighty Days by Jules Verne. Many thanks to LuAnn O'Connell for relating how she and her two daughters did a world geography study using this classic book.

In LuAnn's words:

"Our family found studying Around the World in Eighty Days one summer to be a fun and effective way to study world geography. After all, what other book contains the diversity and adventure of a brisk walk down Pall Mall in London, a steamer voyage through the three-year-old Suez Canal, an elephant ride across the Indian jungle, a leisurely carriage ride in Singapore, conveyance on a palanquin in Hong King, a journey on a steam train attacked by American Indians, a freezing sail on a wind-driven ice sledge across the American prairie, the hijacking of a trading vessel in the Atlantic and a harrowing hansom cab ride through London? Fascinating characters, challenging vocabulary, lessons in time and longitude, map reading, and the events of the Victorian Era rounded out the study covering geography, history, language arts, and math all in eighty days (which is how much time we spent on this study!).

My daughters, Tabitha and Grace, and I used the Whole Story version of this book as the basis of this unit study. This particular version contains side notes giving background information on countries and cities, history and science. As we read, we followed Phileas Fogg's progress on a blank world map, marking the city and date of arrival. My oldest daughter, Tabitha, gained skills in creating tables by making a table of Fogg's itinerary with his projected and actual arrival and departure dates at each city when mentioned in the book. We used the Audio Memory Geography Songs tape and book to learn the countries of the world, concentrating on Asia as we were in the process of adopting a little girl from China at the time. With the computer software World Discovery Deluxe, Grace, Tabitha and I played map quizzes about countries, capitals, major rivers and flags. With the same software we created our own map quiz of questions from the story. For more in-depth study each of us chose on the countries Fogg passed through to give an oral report on, allowing me to teach them outlining, research, and presentation skills.

Most of our activities related in some way to geography. For science, since steam power played such a large role in Fogg's travels, we studied the development of the steam engine and visited a museum with a real steam train. We discussed why the Calcutta to Bengal railroad was longer than the distance the crow flies (mountains) and why the shortest routes for international flights often take planes to northern latitudes, testing this with a string on a globe. (We also got to fly over the North Pole on our flight to China!!)

We learned about three major climate zones of the earth: arctic, temperate, and tropical and used art books to draw animals from each region.

For math related activities, we graphed and compared populations of the largest countries and endeavored to understand Fogg's miscalculation of the length of his journey which resulted from traveling toward the sun.

For language arts, Tabitha and Grace labeled the pictures they had drawn while I read aloud. Tabitha copied dialogue from the book to learn the correct mechanics of writing dialogue and studied vocabulary words used in the story, such as "taciturn" and "tranquil." Also, in the Whole Story version we learned about geographically related word origins -- for instance, "leotards" are named after the nineteenth century French acrobat who invented the flying trapeze and "bungalow" comes from the Hindi word which means "of Bengal." We viewed the TV mini-series of this story, comparing it to the book. (Author's note -- our family began to view the movie version and found it to be unacceptable. We've not found the TV mini-series.)

The culmination of our journey around the world were several international meals Tabitha and I served from countries and regions visited by Phileas Fogg as well as an Around the World in Eighty Days TV show the girls produced themselves. Some of the meals we enjoyed were meatballs and grissini (bread sticks) from Italy and lentil soup and pita bread from the Middle East.

On the night of our French meal featuring French beef soup, homemade French bread and lady fingers, the girls showed their TV show to their grandparents and family. Scenes Tabitha and Grace had drawn from the book and pasted on a scroll were pulled through the cardboard box "TV" as they took turns narrating the story. We had intended to go all the way around the world with our menus, with Navajo tortillas from America and an English tea to celebrate Fogg's return to England, but unlike Phileas Fogg, we ran out of steam in Japan!

Around the World in Eighty Days is such a rich book. There is much that can be studied from it: world religions, transportation, Victorian culture, colonialism, languages, the Suez Canal, Native Americans, India, Japan, advanced map skills, the effect of topography on transportation and population, world travel today, etc. This is an ideal book for a family or support group who wish to study world geography through living books and have fun doing it!"

Writing and Geography

Fifty State Files - Kids Love Mail!

One worthwhile way to learn about the 50 states is to begin a 50 state file. Combining letter writing skills with research, filing, and even some art, this long-term project can culminate in a useful collection of facts, pictures, information and maps.

Challenge: In one year can we collect a map, postcard, or brochure from each of the 50 states?

Materials

- USA wall map
- Expandable file folder or file box
- 50 folders or 50 divider tabs
- Student *50 State Notebook (3 ring binder or composition book)

Help the student craft a letter asking for information and a map, postcard, or brochure about a state. Have the student explain the project simply and ask for exactly what they are looking for. Send letters to the Chamber of Commerce for each state. You can find this information at the library or http://chamber-of-commerce.com/search3.htm

Also, you might try the Chamber of Commerce in some of the bigger cities in each state for additional materials.

In order not to overwhelm the student both in letter writing and in amount of material coming in the mail, stagger your requests to about five per month. This also keeps postage from becoming a big issue. (Additionally, they could send postcards in lieu of letters to save money.)

As material arrives in the mail, the student browses through it and picks out the items of particular interest. Students might want to cut out pictures to copy or tape into their student notebook or on the wall map. Help them decide what's valuable to keep and what might be tossed.

Tip

Predetermine what in particular you'd like to learn about: animals, road maps, weather, state parks, tourist attractions, famous citizens, etc. Teach them how to file away the information.

The Student Notebook of 50 States might also include information that can be collected from a student almanac: state bird, state motto, date of admittance into the union, etc.

The neat thing about the file box is that you can use it for years to come for:

- ❑ Travel information for family or friends -- a goldmine of resources right at your fingertips.
- ❑ Resources for reports as students get older
- ❑ Variety of pictures to cut out and tape to maps or to use in other projects.

Other options

Use the Internet to research the states and print out appropriate information.

Use the public library for books on each of the states, magazine articles, perhaps even videos.

Instead of a file box your student could keep a student notebook with just selected information taped into it.

The Student History Notebook of America has 50 blank pages that would work great as a 50 States Notebook. See Resources.

World File Box

Using the above ideas, write Embassies to collect information about places around the world.

Vocabulary and Geography

Geographic Terms

Aquifer
Atoll
Bay
Biosphere
Bluff
Bog
Butte
Canyon
Cartography
Census
Channel
Civilization
Clouds
Coastal Plain
Conservation
Delta
Deserts
Drought
Dune
Eclipse
Ecosystem
Elevation
Equator
Equinox
Estuary
Fjord
Flood Plain
Fog

Food Chain
Front
Geyser
Glacier
Gorge
Government
Gulf
Habitat
Humidity
Islands
Isthmus
Jet Stream
Key
Lagoon
Landslide
Latitude
Longitude
Levee
Magma
Mantle
Marsh
Mesa
Meteoroid
Migration
Mining
Monsoon
Oasis
Ocean

Peninsula
Permafrost
Plain
Prairie
Precipitation
Prime Meridian
Reservoir
Richter Scale
Ring of Fire
Rocks - 3 types
      igneous
      metamorphic
      sedimentary
Savanna
Sediment
Seismology
Silt
Sinkhole
Solstice
Strait
Swamp
Tides
Time Zones
Topography
Tributary
Tropics
Tsunami
Water Cycle
Wetland

These are just a few of the many geographic terms that children should become familiar with over the years. Many lend themselves well to picture definitions. Try using them in map projects and as part of vocabulary/spelling lists. Other geographic words should be added as you encounter them in life, for example: GPS.

Chapter 10
History and Geography

Mama's Mama

Mama's Mama on a winter's day,
Milked the cows and fed them hay,
Slopped the hogs, saddled the mule,
And got the children off to school,
Did a washing, mopped the floors,
Washed the windows and did some chores,
Cooked a dish of home-dried fruit,
Pressed her husband's Sunday suit,
Swept the parlor, made the bed,
Baked a dozen loaves of bread,
Split some wood and lugged it in,
Enough to fill the kitchen bin,
Cleaned the lamps and put in oil,
Stewed some apples she thought might spoil,
Churned the butter, baked a cake,
Then exclaimed: "For Mercy's Sake,
The calves have got out of the pen!"
Went out and chased them in again,
Gathered the eggs and locked the stable,
Returned to the house and set the table,
Cooked a supper that was delicious,
Afterwards washed all the dishes,
Fed the cat, sprinkled the clothes,
Mended a basket full of hose,
Then opened the organ and began to play,
"When You Come to the End of a Perfect Day."

Author Unknown

How do people adapt to their environment around them? Do you see the connection here between history and geography?! It's possible to teach geography without even realizing it. Of course, maps are naturally a part of both history and geography. But cultural aspects are an important part of geography, also. As you study history, be aware of all the geographic implications and build on them when possible. The next two activities are hands-on projects that help to capture the history/geography cultural connection. These examples are from American history. You can find many more projects that show life in other lands and during other time periods.

Learning about everyday life in early America is interesting and exciting! Think about our country's forefathers: What did they do? How did they live? Learning about our heritage is a valuable pursuit. Making things we take for granted will opens our eyes to what life in early America was really like!

History & Geography
Project # 1

Candle Making

Thomas Tusser wrote in England in the 16th century in his *Directions to Housewifes*:

> *"Wife, make thine own candle,*
> *Spare penny to handle.*
> *Provide for thy tallow ere frost cometh in,*
> *And make thine own candle ere winter begin."*

Background

In early America, housewives had a choice of two methods of making candles. They could make molded candles. To do this, they would use a candle mold, which was a metal object with several hollowed out candle shapes in it. They would place a wick in the mold and pour melted wax around the wick.

The other method, the one you will use, is called "dipped" candles. Housewives in colonial days would most likely never make just one candle at a time; they would have a holder on which several wicks could be suspended at one time. A housewife would probably be making a whole winter's supply at once.

Wax

Beeswax was preferred for candle making in colonial times. Other choices for making candles included animal fats, which were smoky and tended to smell bad, and bayberries, which are waxy berries from the bayberry bush. Bayberries were plentiful, smelled good, and tended to burn slowly and not smoke. The berries were picked in late Fall when they were ripe. They were boiled and the fat that rose to the surface was skimmed off. When the fat congealed it was green. It would then be remelted and made into candles.

Beeswax is made in a honeycomb by bees. It is not as smoky as candles made from animal fat and does not smell bad. Actually, it still smells faintly of the honey. If the beeswax were straight from the honeycomb, it would need to be cleaned.

CAUTION! MELTED WAX IS VERY HOT!

History and Geography Project #1 (continued)

Materials
- 2 plugs of beeswax
- Wick
- Double boiler or saucepan and mug
- 1 cup of ice cold water
- Newspaper to protect the work surface

Directions
1. To make your candle, place your beeswax in a mug and then into the top half of a double boiler; put water in the bottom half. If you don't have a double boiler, put the wax in a mug and place the mug in a small saucepan that is filled with enough water to come about half way up the mug. Boil the water.

2. Melt the wax.

3. Remove from stove.

4. Carefully dip the wick into the melted wax and then into a cup of ice water. Repeat this until your candle is the size and shape you want. If it doesn't turn out right the first time, it's okay! It can be easily melted again and re-dipped.

5. When it is the desired size and shape, it's ready to burn. Pour a little melted wax on a plate and stick your candle to it or cut and trim the bottom to fit into a candle holder. Trim the wick between 1/4" and 1/8".

Tip
Be sure to protect any furniture before burning your candle as it will drip.

Extensions
1. Read about the whaling industry. Certain whales were prized for the material stored in their blunt heads. It was used to make "spermaceti" candles, which are said to have given out more light than three tallow candles combined.

2. Read about other forms of lighting: pine-knots or candlewood, rushes, and many interesting types of lamps. See if you can track down some old lamps. What were they named and how were they used?

Vocabulary
-- Tallow -- Commonly refers to the fat of cattle and sheep, melted and separated for use in candles and soap. A similar fatty substance can be obtained from plants (like bayberries) and is sometimes referred to as tallow, also.

-- Wick -- Back then, wick was commonly made of loosely spun hemp or cotton or milkweed.

History & Geography
Project # 2

Taffy Pulling

Background

Entertainment in early America was vastly different from the world of amusement we live in today; no television, stereos, video tapes, computer games, playgrounds, or the like. People found simpler ways to amuse themselves. One popular form of entertainment consisted of getting together with other folks and making something useful, like a quilt. A taffy pull was that kind of entertainment. It provided a way to socialize, have fun, and make something.

CAUTION! MIXTURE IS VERY HOT!

Materials
- 1 cup sugar
- 3 tablespoons corn starch
- Pinch of salt
- 1/4 cup of water
- 2/3 cup of honey
- Candy thermometer (optional)
- Platter or cookie sheet
- Butter

Directions
1. Grease a platter or cookie sheet thoroughly.
2. Combine sugar, corn starch, and salt with water and honey in a saucepan.
3. Boil until the mixture reaches the "hard ball" stage. (If you are using a candy thermometer, it is 250 - 266 degrees.)
4. If you are not using a candy thermometer, test for the hard ball stage by allowing a few drops of the hot mixture to drop into a cup of cold water. Put your fingers in the cup and try to push the mixture together. If it forms a firm ball, it has reached the "hard ball" stage. If it forms a ball but it is soft, your taffy isn't quite ready yet.

Tip

Watch carefully! It can reach the "hard ball" stage very quickly. If allowed to heat beyond the "hard ball" stage, the mixture will be too hard to form a ball. DO NOT allow it to get to this point.

When the taffy can be formed into a hard ball, pour it onto a well-greased platter or cookie sheet. Allow it to cool at room temperature. (Not in the refrigerator or cold outside air.) Occasionally lift the outer edges into the center to ensure that the taffy cools at a uniform rate.

Pulling

All participants in the taffy pull should thoroughly wash their hands and then butter them. The butter keeps the taffy from sticking to your skin, insulates your hands, and imparts a tasty flavor to the candy! As soon as the taffy can be handled, you should start pulling. Don't wait too long or the taffy will harden and you won't be able to work it.

Take a big glob of taffy from the outside edge (where it is coolest) and begin pulling. Stretch it out as far as it will go, then fold both ends back into the center. Repeat this many times until the taffy is just too hard to stick back together again.

It's fun to work in teams of two people where each team gets a fairly large glob to work with. But it can be accomplished singly as well. The taffy gets "whiter" as it is worked. That is because the pulling is incorporating air into the candy.

When you are done pulling, lay the taffy down and give it the final shape you want it to have. It can be twisted or formed into letters or number. Or it can be left in a long rope and then cut with a knife or scissors into smaller pieces. It is now ready to eat and enjoy!

Extensions

1. Watch for forms of entertainment like taffy pulling and quilting bees in books. What do we do today that is comparable?

2. Plan an old-fashioned evening with family or friends. Cook a meal from the *Little House on the Prairie Cookbook* or one of the American Girls' cookbooks. Use lamplight or candlelight. Make candles, taffy, pomander balls, sew a project, or string popcorn. Read aloud to one another. Learn to play some games from long ago. (Try your library for books about games.)

Timelines

Everything happened some*where* -- hence maps. Everything happened some*time* -- hence timelines. The connection between geography and history is vital. Knowing where something happened is as good as knowing when it happened. However, it is far more valuable to know both pieces of information: where and when. Students will be more likely to retain information that they can place in context.

Habits!

As you teach history, make it a habit to show where events happened as well as when they happened. A simple and highly effective habit is to always have students mark the where on the map and the when on a timeline. For example, as you discuss Christopher Columbus your students will add him to their timeline and mark on the map important information like: place of birth, Spain, and his voyage routes. It is especially memorable if you use the same symbol for Columbus on the timeline that you used on the map. So if you had a small drawing of him that you put on the timeline, put a copy of the same drawing on your map, too. That visual reminder will make the connection of when and where even stronger.

Types of Timelines

For the early elementary ages, a linear timeline is easier to follow. This could be done in a variety of ways:

- ❏ Strips of 8 ½ x 11 paper or posterboard taped along the hallway.
- ❏ Butcher paper rolled out as you need it.
- ❏ Index cards laid out one by one along your table -- and stored in a baggie when not in use.
- ❏ Clothesline hung from one end of the room to another and clothespins used to hang up cards or icons to represent the study.*
- ❏ A laminated linear timeline that is useable over and over again. Bright Ideas Press makes an inexpensive one that works very well for the younger crowd.

*Clothesline Timeline
Directions

1. Have reference books on hand
2. Choose events and time frame
3. Gather icons
4. Make century or decade markers from cardstock and pin to clothesline
5. Hang icons with clothespins
6. Add other times relevant to the kids' frame of knowledge

Timelines (continued)

Exploring Ancient Civilizations? Add Jesus' birth and discovery of America for a frame of reference.

Discovering USA history? Go back in time and add Jesus' birth on one end and go forward and add your student's birthday on the other.

Try to keep the timeline at least nominally to scale. Obviously when doing so some feet of clothesline will be very bare compared to others. This is a great discussion starter -- why is there so much more notable history in some times than others?

Other Questions
- ❑ Why do we have dates for fewer events the farther back in time we go?
- ❑ Of what significance was the printing press?
- ❑ What do B.C. and A.D. really mean?
- ❑ What century were you born in?
- ❑ What century do you live in now?

Don't forget to also refer to the "where of events" as you place them on your timeline.

Some specialty timelines you might enjoy constructing with your kids:
- ❑ Bible stories
- ❑ Famous missionaries
- ❑ Discoveries/Inventions
- ❑ Wars
- ❑ Great composers or artists
- ❑ Presidents
- ❑ Your own family

Warning!
Don't get trapped into the mind set that your timeline has to be really cool or "perfectly" organized!! Many people avoid doing one because they want to do it just "right" and therefore never do it. Simple is fine -- in some ways preferable -- If your expectations are reasonable it is more likely you'll actually get started. If you don't like the first one you do, learn from that and do your second one differently. Some weeks or months you may add a lot to it and other times it may be ignored for awhile. If you can routinely add to it though, you'll find it to be a quietly beneficial activity that only takes a little time to do.

History is Messy!
You'll find conflicting dates and information, you'll find that you can't cram everything in that you'd like, and you'll find out that sometimes history is downright messy! That's okay -- that's the way life really is; God is orderly but mankind is not!

Chapter 11
MAPS GALORE

Activities and Projects

Project #1 - Sticker Geography
Project #2 - Hero Geography
Project #3 - Book Maps
Project #4 - Real Maps in the Real World
Project #5 - 3-D Maps
Project #6 - Geo Terms Map
Project #7 - Current Events
Project #8 - Favorite Book Maps
Project #9 - Imaginary Island
Project #10 - Jigsaw Map
Project #11 - Map Hobbies
Project #12 - Neighborhood Map Activity
Project #13 - More Maps
Project #14 - Mystery Map Ride
Project #15 - Treasure Map
Project #16 - USA Regions

Maps Galore Project #1
Sticker Geography

Kids love stickers! Stickers provide great visual interest to map projects. There's an amazing variety of inexpensive stickers available. Keep your eye out for those that may come in useful in your studies. Collect sticker packs as you travel. When we were in Arizona we found both iguana and tarantula stickers. Look for tiny little star and dot stickers at teacher supply stores. (Great for denoting capitol cities, travel, important places, etc.) Museum gift shops often sell unique stickers and of course, craft stores usually have a wide selection.

Stickers can be pulled out as needed to spice up your history or science maps or a "Sticker Map" can be your primary focus. Here are several "Sticker Map" ideas:

Tip
Stickers don't come off of laminated surfaces easily! Paper maps might be preferable for these activities.

Materials
- USA Outline Map
- Variety of "Place" or "Travel" stickers
- Atlas, almanac, reference material

Directions
Working with the stickers you have on hand, have students decide what place or event each sticker might represent. For example, a horse sticker might represent the Pony Express. Add some tiny dots to show its route. Or a horse might represent cavalry in the Civil War. Train stickers could be used for the Transcontinental Railroad or a canoe for Lewis and Clark. Native American style stickers can be used to denote a variety of tribes or current reservations as well as important historical events like the Trail of Tears.

Tip
Can't find just the right sticker? Make your own by cutting out pictures or drawing what you need and attaching it with two-sided tape.

Variations
- ❏ Food stickers -- crops grown, regional dishes, foods from earlier time periods
- ❏ Boats -- exploration, trade, and naval battles
- ❏ Animals -- habitats, Lewis & Clark's expedition, migration
- ❏ Plants -- cactus for the southwest, etc.
- ❏ Stars or dots -- original 13 colonies, capitols, trails & routes,
- ❏ Balloons -- birthplace of presidents or relatives
- ❏ There are even historic landmark stickers available -- Statue of Liberty, etc.

Sticker Geography (continued)

Naturally, a sticker map can be made for any area of the world you wish to study. Just use the appropriate map and reference materials.

Using a sticker you already have and deciding what it represents frees the imagination as well as gives you a great excuse to pull out and use a variety of reference materials as you strive to find the right place or event for each sticker!

The final map will make a great addition to any wall -- sure to be admired by all who see it -- and a great reminder to the kids about everything they learned while compiling their Sticker Map!

Maps Galore Project #2
Hero Geography

Everyone needs heroes! Children especially need great role models in their lives. People of noble character and great deeds inspire us to do our best also. Who are your children's heroes? Who are yours? Choose five or ten heroes. They could be Bible heroes, heroes of the faith, missionaries, great leaders, astronauts, or everyday heroes like grandparents, police and firemen, etc. Where were these heroes born or where was their sphere of influence? Pick a map to use that would work best for your hero study. (For some, like missionaries, you may wish to use a world map in addition to other maps.)

Materials
- Map(s) to write on
- Color pencils or markers
- Atlas
- Reference materials

Directions
1. Learn about your heroes.
2. Assign each hero a color and color in their birth place and areas of influence
3. Make a Key (see below)

Key
Make a key explaining the colors for each person. The key should be located in an area of the map not being utilized for this study. (For example, pick an area of the ocean that isn't needed.) Write in each heroes name in the color you used on the map for that person. You might also draw a picture of the person (or an icon that represents them next to their name in the key. For explorers, military heroes, and great statesmen, their nation's flag would make a great addition. If your heroes traveled, don't forget to draw in their travels in their own color. Decide what symbol denotes travel and mark it in your key (i.e., green is for Amy Carmichael and little green footprints show where she traveled).

Keep this project fun and inspirational -- watch movies about your heroes, read interesting books, pretend to be them for the day! Use lots of color and the students' great ideas on this map -- hang the map as a poster when finished.

Maps Galore Project #3
Book Maps - A Book List with Pizzazz!

Read a good book lately? Probably. Have your students added it to their map? This is such fun -- and you end up with a colorful and exciting "Book List" in the form of a map rather than a plain old reading log.

Keep a large paper outline map just for books read. This can be a family map or each student might like to have their own. You can add to it for years! You might even want two -- a USA and a world map.

Every book takes place somewhere. Even fictional books have a setting -- whether real or imaginary. Some books lend themselves well to tracking the action on a map while reading the story. Use a sticker or drawing to represent the main character(s) and little dots to show where they traveled.

Other books may be added to the map after you've finished reading them. Draw a picture of a favorite scene, draw an icon that reminds you of the story, design a book cover or cut out pictures that represent the book. Add a picture to the map in the place most associated with the story. For example, a student might draw a picture of a silver goblet and place it near Boston to show he has read *Johnny Tremain*. If there is important travel in the book you can add that with little tiny dots.

Or add a key or legend in a corner somewhere to show what your pictures represent. For example, you put a silver goblet near Boston. The key would show the same picture, perhaps smaller, then the words "Johnny Tremain -- growing up during the American Revolution" and perhaps the name of the author as well. (You might want to place your key in the Atlantic Ocean where there is more room to make a drawing to represent the book.) Boston would then be colored in. At the end of the year your student will have a map that shows each book they've read that year -- way cooler than a plain old book list!

Maps Galore Project #4
Real Maps in the Real World

Introduce young children to simplified maps. If you can't find a map of your neighborhood or town, make your own. Some places to look for simple maps: Tourist offices, Chambers of Commerce, mall maps are often simple, Parks and Recreation maps, libraries. Help your child refer to the map and actually use it to "find" places on a regular basis. As the student matures and their map-reading abilities improve you can use more detailed, complex maps. Please don't frustrate them by trying to use maps that are too difficult for them. Map reading is a more complicated skill to learn than it might appear. Patience and practice pay off here in a desire to read and learn more about maps because it is fun, not frustrating!

When your student is ready, use a clear and easy-to-read city map to plan trips to the grocery store, library, church, etc. Have him highlight places on the map that are important in his life. Then he can highlight the best routes to use to get there.

Use this map occasionally as you run your errands with your young geographer helping you to follow it. Regular map usage will go a long way towards creating map-literate kids. Once they have a good grasp of the city map, invite them to help you plan longer trips using state or regional maps.

Although world maps are certainly important, finding Madagascar does not have the same connection to a seven-year-old as finding her way to her dad's office! Expose them to a variety of maps. Use real life occasions to consult a variety of maps: bus routes, mall maps, relief maps, weather maps, historical maps, etc.

Keep maps up on the walls of your home. One on the dining room or kitchen table covered with a clear plastic table cloth will go a long way towards promoting daily map reading. There are neat map shower curtains, posters, and "kid friendly" maps available with which you may plaster bedroom, bathroom, and school room walls. Backs of doors and ceilings are other fun places to stick maps. We rotate our maps and use a variety of styles, colors, sizes, areas, etc. to maintain interest and keep on learning new things. Old *National Geographic* magazines, widely available at yard sales everywhere, are great for special interest maps. We love the maps of whales and dolphins, ocean floors, the solar system, historical journeys, and the many others we have had posted in our home.

Of course, maps are flat and our world is certainly not. It does help to have a globe handy to teach about hemispheres, latitudes and longitudes, orbits, etc. Buy an inexpensive one at a big discount store during the summer back-to-school sales. Can your kids find the Equator, Prime Meridian, the South Pole, their state, and the continents?

Wide exposure to maps opens up the world!

Maps Galore Project #5
3-D Maps

Creating a tabletop map with items from your home makes a great hands-on project with strong visual appeal. Use a card table set up for this purpose as you'll want to allow at least a few days to work on it and several more to admire the finished outcome.

Materials
- Table
- Atlases & Maps
- Stickers
- Index Cards
- Icons -- some examples: Legos, clay, pipe cleaners, play mobile figures, farm animals, plastic people, Lincoln Logs, boats, trains, cars, little houses, forts, plants, and dollhouse miniature items.
- Posterboard
- Foam Board
- Tape
- Toothpicks
- Plasti Tak

Directions
1. Decide on your study - what will the map represent? Ideas: Family Tree, Animal Habitats, 13 Colonies, Exploration, Ancient Civilizations, Westward Expansion, Weather or Volcanoes, Missionary Journeys, etc.

2. Draw a map on the poster board depicting the area necessary for your study. Don't worry about it being perfect or even to scale for this project! For example, let's say you are concentrating on the 13 Colonies. Draw in the whole USA, but make the 13 Colonies much bigger. Add a smallish Atlantic Ocean and the edge of Europe to show from whence Explorers and Pilgrims, etc. came.

3. Tape the posterboard map to foam board.

4. Use the Plasti Tak to affix the small icons to the map on appropriate places.

5. Write a concise explanation of the person, place or event on each index card. Cut the index card as small as possible. Tape it to a toothpick and stick it next to the area to which it is referring.

Tip
Cut into the foam board to have "pop-ups" about places or extra tidbits of information that don't fit elsewhere.

Maps Galore Project #6
Geo Terms Map

Collect pictures from magazines that depict geographic terms (deserts, plains, volcanoes, bays, etc.). Tape them to the appropriate place on a world map. This is a map that can be added to all year. Or do this in a notebook along with the geographic terms your students are defining.

For example, the student defines "plateau" in his notebook. Then he draws a picture or cuts out a picture of a plateau and tapes it to the appropriate place on his map. (Where would one find a plateau?) The picture becomes a visual reminder for the word he has just learned.

Maps Galore Project #7
Current Events

Materials
- Large wall map
- Small stickers, pins with color heads, or Post-It Notes™ Flags
- News sources

Directions
At the beginning of the school year, hang a large world map somewhere very accessible. You may prepare an inexpensive paper map on which kids can attach stickers or you might use a laminated map and Post-It Note™ Flags.

Every day make a point of discussing one place mentioned in that days' news. Children find the spot on the map and mark it. Review the marked places weekly. At the end of each month, see how many current events can be recalled just from looking at the map. By the end of the year, many different places and events will have been covered. The hands-on aspect of marking the places coupled with the reviews ensure greater retention of the information discussed.

Optional
You may like for older studnets to keep a Current Events Notebook, in which they briefly jot down the name of the place and a one sentence synopsis of the news relevancy.

Maps Galore Project #8
Favorite Book Maps

Remember the Book Map idea on page 87? Unlike that activity which results in map that depicts where each book you've read takes place, this project maps out the plot of one specific book.

Directions

1. Pick a book your child has enjoyed hearing read or has read himself.

2. Decide on the type of map to draw. Some books lend themselves well to a map showing the main character's travels (*Around the World in Eighty Days*, *Hans Brinker or the Silver Skates*, biographies of Daniel Boone or Christopher Columbus). Other books are best served by drawing a map of the area in which it takes place (*Little House on the Prairie* or *Little Britches* series). Still other books may be best depicted by mapping important events in the story (*Johnny Tremain*). Non-fiction, historical fiction, autobiographies, and biographies work best. Fiction may be used if you'd like your child to draw a map of what the setting "looks" like based on the description in the book.

3. If you choose a book that is set in a real locale, an atlas or other reference will be necessary.

4. If the book takes place in a fictional land, begin with the first and take notes of geographical details and travel references.

5. Using these notes and your child's imagination, draw, color, and label your map. This is fun to do on an oversize piece of cardstock or posterboard.

Note

Children who complete this project learn quickly that they must listen and watch carefully for geographical information. This attention to detail will improve their overall comprehension level!

Maps Galore Project #9
Imaginary Island

Materials
* Paper
* Pencil/markers

Directions
Tell your child to pretend they've just discovered an Imaginary Island! Now they need to name it and draw it. Here are some points to consider, bearing in mind the age and ability of the student:

1. Where is their island located on the world map or globe?
2. What is its longitude and latitude?
3. What is its topography?
4. What plants grow there?
5. What animals and/or insects live there?
6. What is the weather like?

This is a great way to introduce terms such as:
- ☐ topography
- ☐ latitude/longitude
- ☐ climate

Encourage your students to fill in the appropriate items:
1. Compass Rose
2. Key/Legend
3. Physical features such as rivers and mountains
4. Older students may be able to add Scale, also.

Optional
Some children will enjoy writing or telling a story about this island, how it was discovered and what was found there. Have them think about how the physical features and climate affected the plants, animals, people, etc. living there. It's fun to draw a country flag, make up money, and even choose a form of government.

Maps Galore Project #10
Jigsaw Map

Materials
- Photocopy of a map
- Tracing Paper
- Color pencils or markers
- Contact paper (optional)
- Tag board or cardstock
- Gluestick
- Scissors

Directions
1. Trace a state, country, or continent*
2. Label it
3. Color it
4. Glue it to the cardstock
5. Cover it with contact paper for sturdiness (optional)
6. Cut it out into pieces. Younger students may cut their map into just a few pieces, older students might prefer to cut their map into many pieces. For example, the United States could be cut into regions or into individual states.
7. Put the jigsaw map together!

Tips
Map a jigsaw map collection. Store each map in a labeled zipped bag. Three-hole punch the bags and store in a three-ring binder. Or use a shoe box. Encourage regular play with the maps.

Older children can make maps for their younger siblings or friends. Trade maps.

By tracing, labeling, coloring, cutting and assembling these maps, the kids better remember the shapes and names of the places being studied.

*Use the continent maps in the back of this book.

Maps Galore Project #11
Map Hobbies

Materials
- Newspaper
- Map
- Paper & pencil

Directions
Choose a favorite hobby. Keep you eye out for newspaper or magazine articles related to this hobby. Pick interesting ones! Read the article yourself and see what tie in to geography you can find. Then read it aloud to your student.

Discuss it with them. Ask "why" questions. For example, "Why do the Atlanta Braves have spring training in Kissimmee? Where is Kissimmee anyway?" (Hint, think weather!)

This requires more involvement on your part than many of the other activities in this book. Older readers can watch for interesting items themselves but for the most part the adult is going to be the one to dig up cool stuff about a hobby and make the effort to see the geography connection.

The side benefit to this is the time spent together in a pleasurable activity (which is why it's important to pick a hobby the child likes!) with your child. When the interest wears off, move on to other things. Beating dead horses is a sure cure for enthusiasm!

Creative teachers are good at finding ways to bring children's interests into the classroom. Obviously, geography is just one example of a subject that can be integrated with hobbies. Math, English, art, etc. can also be used.

Maps Galore Project #12
Neighborhood Map Activity

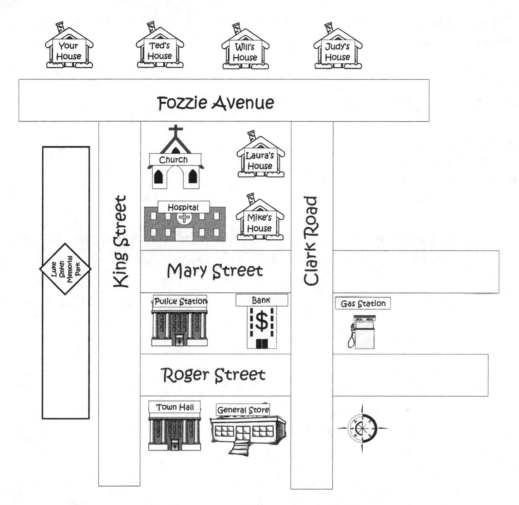

Directions

1. Using the above map, answer the following questions and plot them on the map.

2. What road do you take to get from your house to Laura's house?

3. Name all of the buildings south of the Church.

4. Ted wants to get a book from the Library and bring it to Mrs. Helms at the Hospital. What route should he take?

5. What would be the fastest way to get to the Town Hall from Will's house?

6. What road is between the Gas Station and the Bank?

7. Whose houses are on Clark Street?

8. When looking west from between Laura's and Mike's house, what two buildings would you most easily see?

Maps Galore Project #13
More Maps

Use this activity after your child has done other mapping projects and has a basic understanding of different types of maps.

Materials
- Tracing paper
- Atlas
- Encyclopedia
- Other reference books
- Color pencils or markers

Directions
1. Trace or photocopy several copies of the same map. You might prefer to use a country or continent related to your history studies.

2. Using the reference material, fill in each map with one of the following topics:

   a. animals
   b. population
   c. religions
   d. language
   e. imports/exports
   f. physical features
   g. climate
   h. other?

3. After doing several different kinds of maps of the same place, have the student display them on a poster board. What can he tell you about that place now? What kinds of deductions can he make about life there from reading these thematic maps?

Tip
By doing a number of maps about the same region, your child is learning what information different kinds of maps contain as well as becoming very familiar with the region itself.

Maps Galore Project #14
Mystery Map Ride

Learning to read maps is an important life skill, one that many adults unfortunately have never conquered. Teaching this skill to youngsters is very rewarding but plan on spending time working on it over the years. Be patient. Start very simply and don't move on until the child has a good grasp of the information. It's important to be patient and systematic. Pushing the child to try and read road maps without the skills necessary to do so is expecting them to do Algebra without having learned basic arithmetic! Here are some steps to take in teaching map-reading skills:

1. Introduce children to skills via a few good workbook style pages, draw your own, or use one of the outline maps in this book.

2. Terminology is very important. Left, right, straight, before, after, etc. must all be understood before moving on to east, west, etc.

3. Illustrate the idea of icons. The drawn picture of a bed stands for the bed. The single tree or two might stand for a whole grove. Even non-readers can decipher simple maps drawn with good icons.

4. Draw maps of the child's home environment to use in simple treasure hunt games. Once he understands these kinds of maps he might enjoy drawing them himself.

5. When the very simple map is mastered, move on to slightly more complicated maps involving backyards or neighborhoods. Use each new map several times until you're sure the child is confident in the use of it.

6. Eventually, you'll work your way up to the "Mystery Map Ride." This can be done as a "Mystery Map Walk" first, only going to the car ride when you're sure your student has a good chance for success.

Materials
*   Homemade map or written directions
*   Transportation

Directions
Using a real road map as a guide, draw a simple map from your house to a "secret" destination. (It could be to the park, the library, a friend's home, or anywhere that suits your fancy!)

The kids become the navigators. They read the map and give the directions. You might start out with a walking mystery map excursion before working up to a car ride. In the car, the kids will need to direct you when to turn, etc. This isn't easy! (How many adults do we know that are good at this?) But by starting out with simple, uncomplicated trips and using this "game" often, your students will become able map readers and navigators -- an important life skill!

Mystery Map Ride (continued)

Variation
A friend used this idea for a Mystery Bike Ride. She "planted" a special treat along the way. When they navigated their bikes correctly to a friend's house they found a coupon taped to the front door with a lunch date and play time with their friends!

Tip
After you and your children have had good success with this in your neighborhood and town introduce them to real road maps and allow them to guide you with it on longer outings. (I met a man once who let his two teenagers do all the navigation on a road trip across country. They took him three days out of the way but he never corrected them. They learned from their mistakes and are much more careful map readers now!)

Maps Galore Project #15
Treasure Map

Tackle this activity after you have introduced and practiced mapping skills and terminology. This is a good hands-on way to see where your child needs direction in understanding map concepts.

Materials
- Treasure to bury (pack of gum, book mark, coins, etc.)
- Paper and pencils or markers
- Measuring tape (optional)
- Compass (optional)

Directions
Pick a spot to bury or hide a treasure -- this becomes " X." Choose a starting place -- "You are here." Draw a map from "You are here" to "X." Add physical features such as rocks, trees, houses, etc. Use a compass rose, legend/key, and perhaps a scale. The older and more experienced student will benefit from a more complicated map than the beginner.

Watch the student follow the map. Only help when actually necessary. Give them time to work it out but keep the frustration level at a minimum. Pay attention to their trouble spots. Are they having difficulties because they are rushing to get the treasure or are they encountering information they haven't learned how to process?

Variation
Write down the directions instead of drawing a map. For example: "From our front porch, go outside and walk 20 feet east. At the oak tree, head north for 5 feet."

Tip
Work with your student and together draw a treasure map for a friend or dad to follow. This gives practice in understanding directions, legends, scale, and in thinking through a problem.

Maps Galore Project #16
USA Regions

Materials
- Enlarged photocopy of a student map of USA regions (page 103)
- Encyclopedia, children's atlas or other reference book about the USA
- Color pencils or markers
- Contact paper (optional)
- Cardboard (optional)

Directions
1. Photocopy map, enlarge it if at all possible.

2. Pick one region. Learn about what makes it a region. What is the climate like? What are the natural resources? What is it known for growing or making?

3. Look up each state in that region. What is its capital? Find one other place of interest in the state to learn about, i.e. Yellowstone National Park, the Statue of Liberty, etc.

4. Pick a geographical feature of each state to study. Rivers, lakes, mountains, deserts, etc. Draw these features on the map. Add them to the legend or key.

5. After you have finished your study, glue stick the map to a piece of cardboard, cover it with clear contact paper, and hang it on the wall!

Tip
This same idea could be applied to whatever part of the world you'd like to study. Divide the continent into countries or a country into regions and learn about them one section at a time.

Or use this activity for a state study. See resources on buying individual, laminated state maps.

Chapter 12
Teaching through the Five Themes of Geography

This section explores each of the five themes and gives suggested ways to teach these themes. It isn't necessary for the students to memorize these themes; they are given for the teacher's benefit. After reading more about the five themes, you'll more easily recognize geographic teaching opportunities as they arise.

Five Themes:

Theme 1 - Location
Position on the Earth's surface

Theme 2 - Place
Physical and Human characteristics. What makes it special? Soil, temperature, rivers, historical events? People -- how are they affected by the characteristics of the place? Their language, government, architecture, industries all help define the unique characteristics of a place.

Theme 3 - Relationships within Places
Humans and their environments

Theme 4 - Movement
People interacting on Earth

Theme 5 - Regions
How they form and change

The following pages include tips and ideas for teaching about the five themes of geography.

Theme 1 - Location

Just as you taught your children "above" and "below," "on" and "under," teach them other important positional words like: left, right, north, and south. Words that describe features like size and shape are necessary, too.

Activities for Teaching Directions

1. Hot & Cold becomes North & South! Play the old "hot & cold" game with a twist. One person picks an object in the room and the other player(s) must try to guess what was chosen by walking around and listening to directions. As a player gets closer to the object the person who chose the object says things like "You're getting warmer, continue heading south." or "You're getting colder, turn right."

2. Treasure Hunts can be simple or complicated. For a quick and easy Treasure Hunt game hide a little treat somewhere in the house or yard. Walk with the players as they look and give them little hints like "Go four more paces and turn left" (or perhaps "east" for an older child). "It's under something big and brown." "Walk to the hall closet and then turn right." "Go behind the garage and then walk due north." Use hints that are age appropriate. Take the time to teach new concepts as you play.

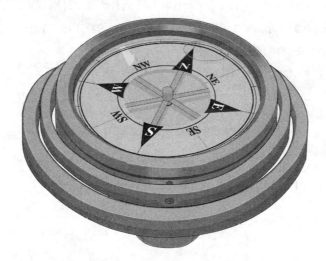

Theme 2 - Place

Discovery Walk

Spend some time walking around your neighborhood. What are some of its characteristics? Things you might watch for include:

- ❏ Plants
- ❏ Animals
- ❏ Soil
- ❏ Climate
- ❏ Types and designs of buildings

Questions to Consider

1. How are the people living here affected by the characteristics of this place?

2. In what ways are this place similar to other places your student is familiar with? In what ways is it different?

3. Read stories with vivid descriptions of life in faraway lands. Watch good videos set in foreign places. Compare and contrast these locations to your own city or town.

Climate

Climate is a wonderful connection between science and geography. Climate certainly affects the characteristics of a place. Can your student think of examples? (i.e., heat/cold can determine clothing styles/choices, types of crops, housing, and if it is a desirable place to live.) The amount of sun/rain/snow, the wind, humidity, and even the likelihood of severe weather (hurricanes, tornadoes, blizzards, etc.) all affect the characteristics of a place.

Weather or Not

Watch the weather on the news, local, national and even worldwide. Learn the terminology. Look at weather maps in the newspaper or off the Internet. Make your own weather map. Learn to identify cloud types. What is necessary to know in order to forecast weather? Begin a forecast chart -- compare yours to the weatherman's. Who needs to know the weather? Do you know a farmer, pilot, or sailor who regularly watches and forecasts the weather -- if so, talk to him and ask questions about their skill and knowledge.

What physical characteristics in your area affect the weather?

Learn about barometers, rain gauges, and other weather-related devices. Use a good weather book to do science experiments related to weather. *Over Our Heads in Wonder -- Science and the Sky* is a wonderful book that ties together Biblical principles and scripture verses with weather-related activities.

Theme 3 - Relationships within Places

How do people adjust to and modify their environment to suit their needs?

Activity -- In the Home

Arrange furniture according to the shape of the room, outlets, and how the room is to be used. Make a floor plan of your home. Cut out furniture pieces from construction paper and arrange them on graph paper sectioned into the rooms of your home.

Tip

This is not easy! Young students will need considerable help in graphing a room on paper. As you work with them, you can be discussing math principles as well as the challenges cartographers face as they try to represent our three-dimensional world on paper!

Activity -- In the Yard

Make a map of your yard. How have you modified the environment there? Planted shade trees? Weeded? Mowed? Cut down trees or bushes? Dug a pond, paved an area for a basketball court, added a screened porch or a bird feeder?

Activity

Look for pictures in books or magazines of how people have shaped their environment. For example: cliff dwellers like the Anasazi in the Southwest as well as the "cliff dwellers" living in ocean front towns of southern California today.

Irrigation, reservoirs, dams, building in difficult places, fencing for animal pastures are all examples of ways man has changed his environment. Some ways in which man has adapted to his environment: houses on stilts, building roads around mountains, and wearing protective clothing in the desert.

Make a chart or collage showing ways in which man has changed or adapted to his environment. Or cut out the pictures and paste them into a geography scrapbook.

Theme 4 - Movement

The patterns of movement of people, products, and information influence the way we learn about geography. We depend on other places for much of our food, clothing, and other items. We share information with others -- communication.

Travel Activity

Provide opportunities for different ways in which to travel: bus rides, subway, train, boat, foot, bike, horse, or ferry.

Clothes Hunt

Do a clothing hunt in your home. Look at the "made in" labels and then mark that country on a map. Who has clothing made from the farthest away? Who has clothing made on an island? Sneakers are good for this game, too.

Food Chain

Trace lunch back to its origins. Make a chart showing from where each ingredient may have originated. Why did your bananas come from Central America but not your milk and eggs? How did the food get to your home? What kinds of foods did your grandparents eat? Why? What are some of the reasons we have such an incredible variety of foods available to us today?

The Name Game

What are the names of some of your students' ancestors? Where were they born? Where did they die? Did they leave their birthplace? Why? How did they travel?

Movement of Information

Brainstorm ways in which ideas and information are presented. (From obvious forms like books and newspapers to less obvious ones like graffiti, bumper stickers, and posters.) Discuss ways your kids communicate with others. Consider these questions and others:

1. How would you get out a message that your ship was under attack?
2. How would you get out a message that you've discovered a cure for the cold?
3. How would you get out a message that a political candidate has something important to say?
4. How would you get out a message that you were having a birthday party?
5. How do people around the world communicate?

Theme 4 - Movement (continued)

License Plate Bingo

Watch for license plates from other states as you travel or just drive around town. Do you see a pattern where you live for cars from out of state? (i.e., "snow birds" heading south for the winter, rural folks coming into town to shop on Fridays, summer beach traffic, etc.)

Theme 5 - Regions

Regions are used to describe a smaller portion of the earth -- an area in which the places have something in common.

The two basic categories are **physical** and **cultural**. **Physical regions** are defined by: land forms, climate, plants, and soil. **Cultural regions** are defined by traits like languages, religions, politics, industry, etc.

What's the difference between a region and a place? West Palm Beach is a place. The Southern United States is a region.

Look at both on a map. Compare and contrast places to regions.

Cities have regions within their boundaries:
- ❑ Residential
- ❑ Commercial
- ❑ Recreational

Regions can be defined by common denominators like:
- ❑ agricultural: The Breadbasket of Europe
- ❑ culture: Latin America or Lapland
- ❑ language: The Arab World
- ❑ historic context: the Original 13 Colonies
- ❑ climate: Rainforests

Other examples of regions are: Central Park, The Gold Coast, Appalachia, Silicon Valley, The Balkans, Normandy, Scandinavia, Indo-China.

Activity
Divide your state, city or neighborhood into regions. Read about other cultures and the regions in which they flourish.

Make a map of the world using regions instead of countries. How many different regions can you think of?

Chapter 13
OUTLINE MAPS

Outline Maps #1
Bright Ideas for Using Outline Maps

Of course, outline maps are great for labeling all sorts of political and physical features: bodies of water, rivers, mountain ranges, cities, states, capitals, countries, continents, longitude, latitude, etc. Here are some other great ideas!

1. Birthplace of US Presidents.
2. Inventors and inventions.
3. Famous composers.
4. Famous or favorite authors.
5. Famous artists.
6. Use your maps as a book list. Plot the story's location.
7. Where are your missionaries? Pray for them.
8. Imports and exports. Where did your pj's come from? How about your coffee?
9. How many US military bases can you find?
10. Which countries forbid Christianity? Plot the persecuted church. Pray for them.
11. Use different colors to show the three major world religions. (Christianity, Judaism, Islam)
12. Match the flag with the country.
13. Write in as many foreign greetings as you can discover (i.e. Aloha! Ciao! Bon Jour!).
14. Follow the concert tour of your favorite band.
15. Trace your ancestors' trek to the "New World".
16. International cuisine. What's Babka? Where did the hamburger come from? Bruschetta? Tiramisu?
17. Where do all your cousins live?
18. Visit the zoo (or your favorite zoo book). Where do all the animals live? Cut out or draw pictures and stick on map.
19. Follow the migratory patterns of bees, butterflies, birds or waterfowl.
20. How many songs can you think of that mention cities, states, or countries? Do you know the way to San Jose? I left my heart… My kind of town, Chicago is…
21. Follow the schedule of your favorite sports team.
22. Note the location of natural disasters. Floods, earthquakes, tornadoes, hurricanes, forest fires.
23. Where do the trees grow? Note the native areas of Ponderosa pines, palm trees, eucalyptus, mahogany, ebony, bamboo etc.
24. Plot as many dormant and active volcanoes as you can. Where's the Ring of Fire?
25. Go on a scavenger hunt around your house. How many geographical locations can you place on your maps? Check the record companies on your CDs, the publishers of your books. Read the labels on the back of your toothpaste, shampoo, etc. Where was your lunch made? How about the peanut butter, the jelly, the bakery, the chips, the banana, the dairy, and the plate you are using.
26. Paste stickers or pictures of different dog breeds and their country of origin.
27. Pick your favorite Olympic event. From which countries do the athletes come?
28. Make a climate or weather map.
29. Topographical maps: what areas are above the mile mark? How many people live below sea level?
30. Where are the rain forests? The deserts?
31. Section your USA or North American maps by Native American Tribes.
32. Do a demographic study map.
33. Current events.
34. The 10/40 window. Pray, pray, pray.
35. Make a cool National Parks map.
36. Trace your summer vacation. Make your own road atlas. If you flew on an airplane, mark all the places you missed.
37. Voyages of discovery. Chart the course of the explorers.
38. How did Lewis and Clark get to the Pacific?
39. Where was the Oregon Trail?
40. Trace Route 66.
41. Where were/are the mining towns? The Gold rush?
42. Label Jesus' ministry and Paul's journeys.
43. Draw in famous landmarks – the Eiffel Tower, Statue of Liberty, Hanging Gardens of Babylon, etc.
44. Can you think of more?

North America

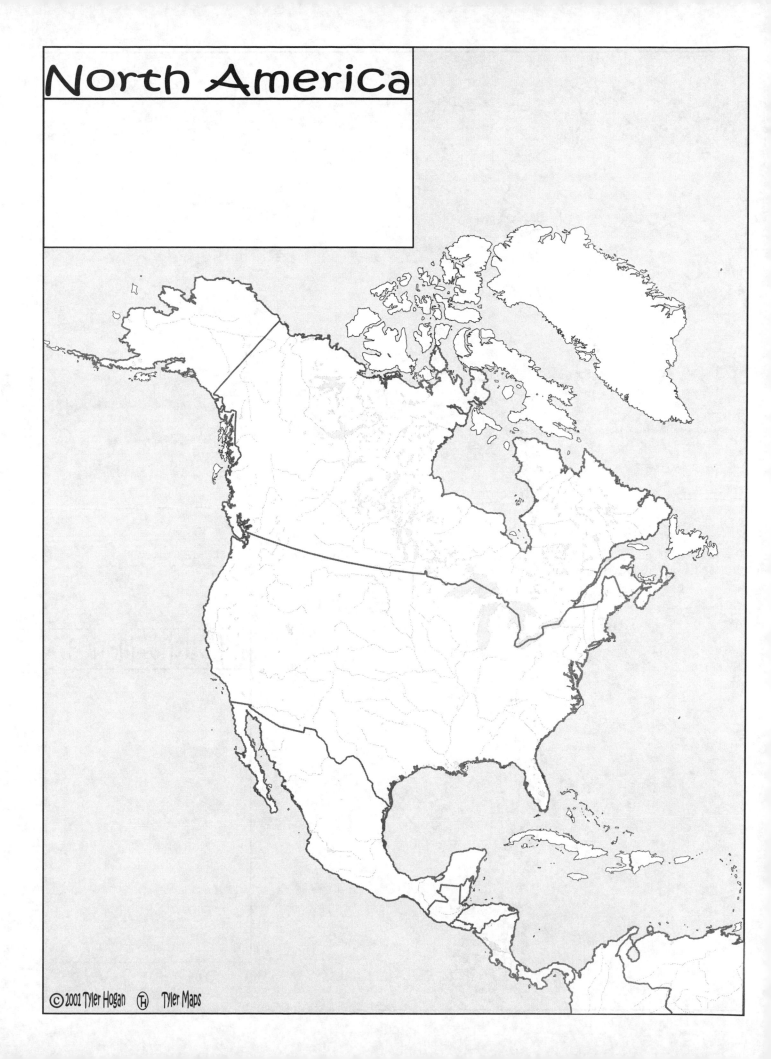

South America

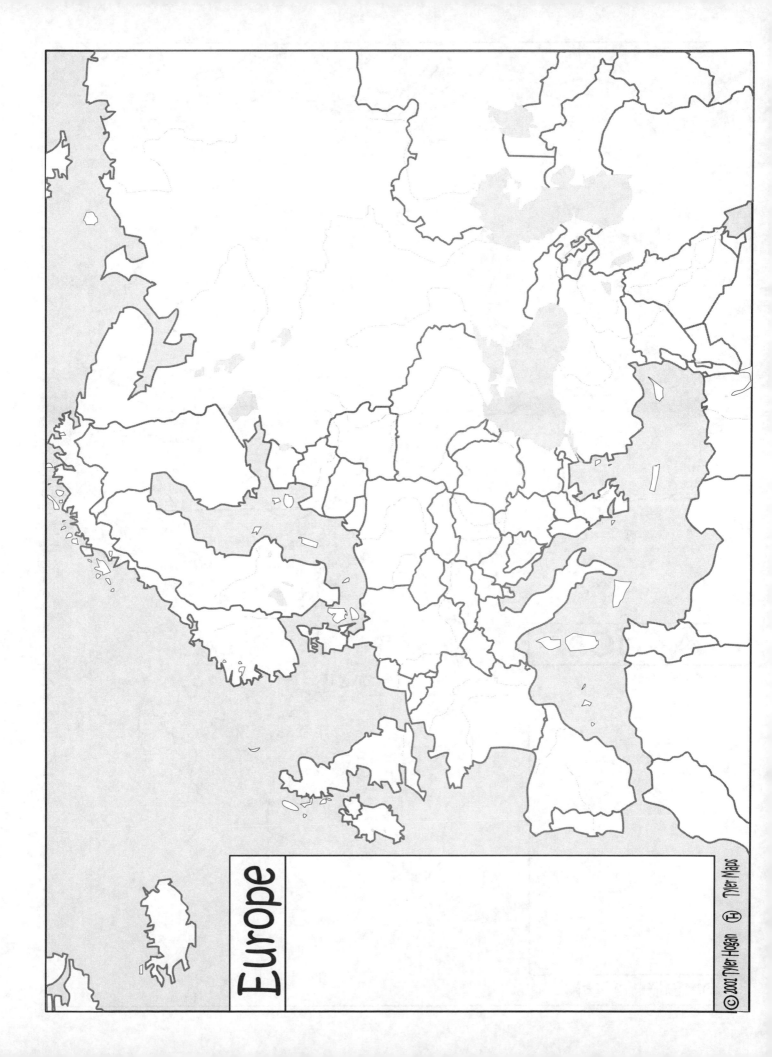

Europe

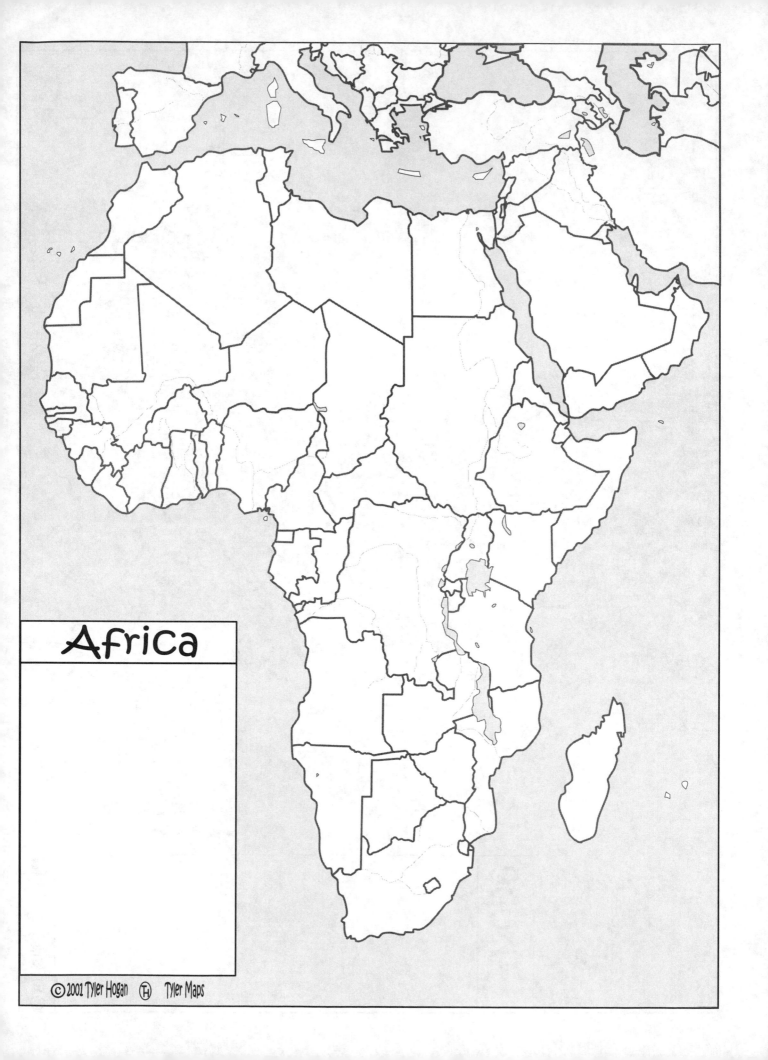

Africa

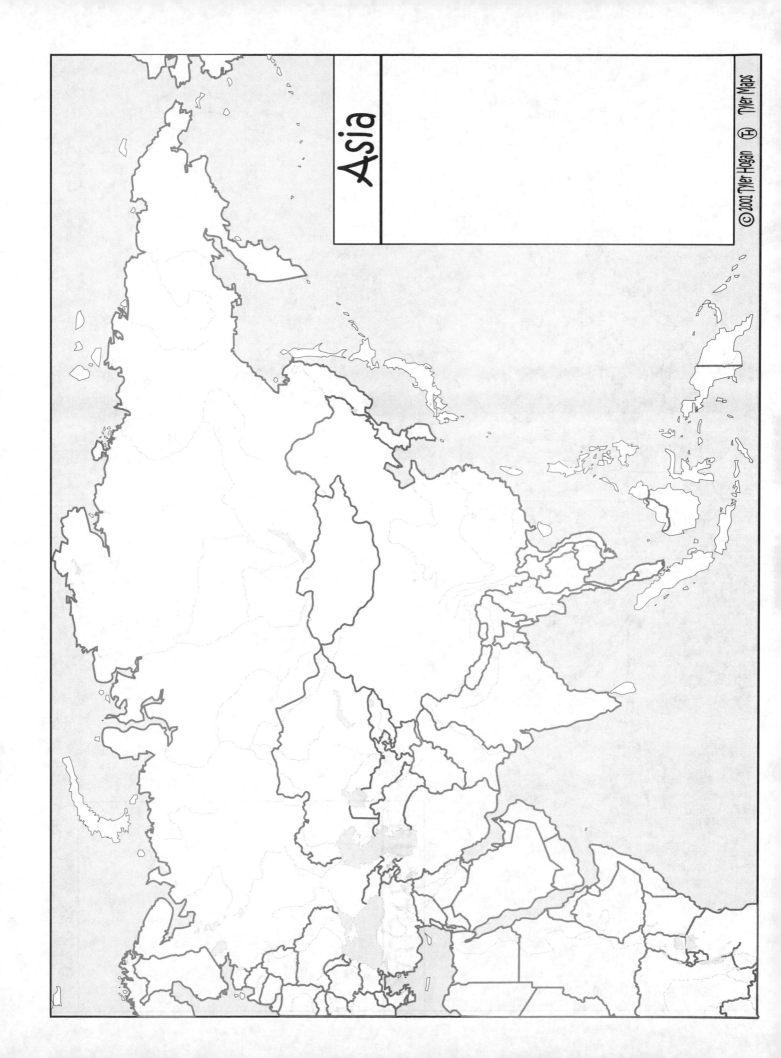

Asia

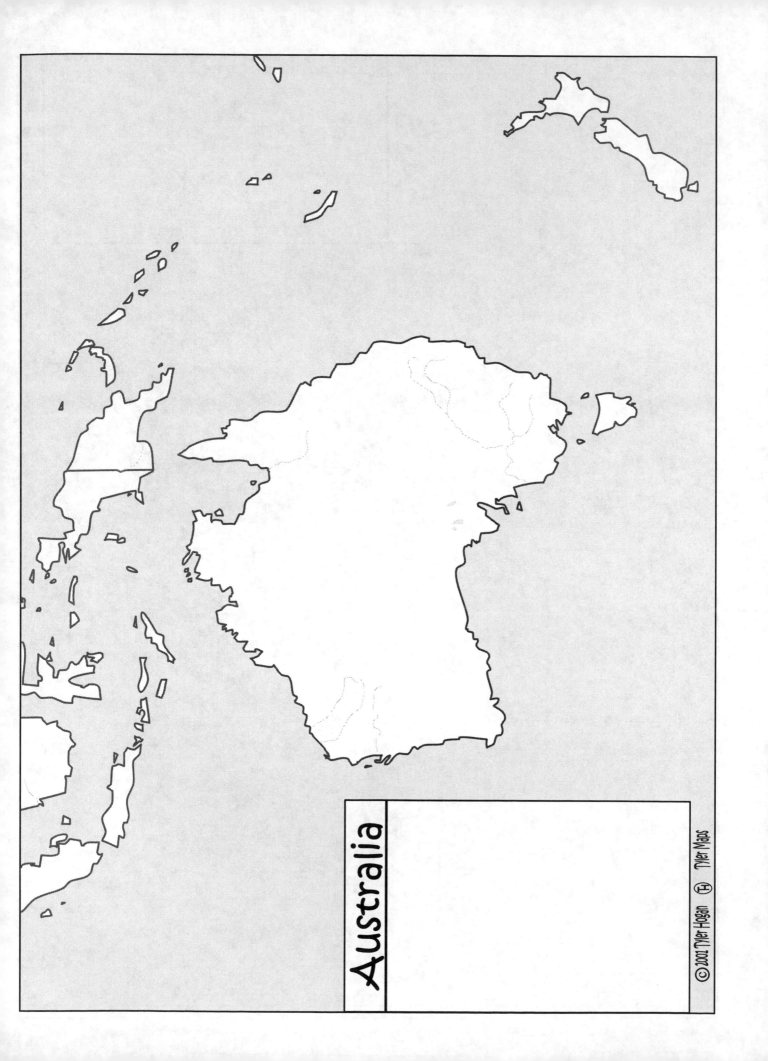

Australia

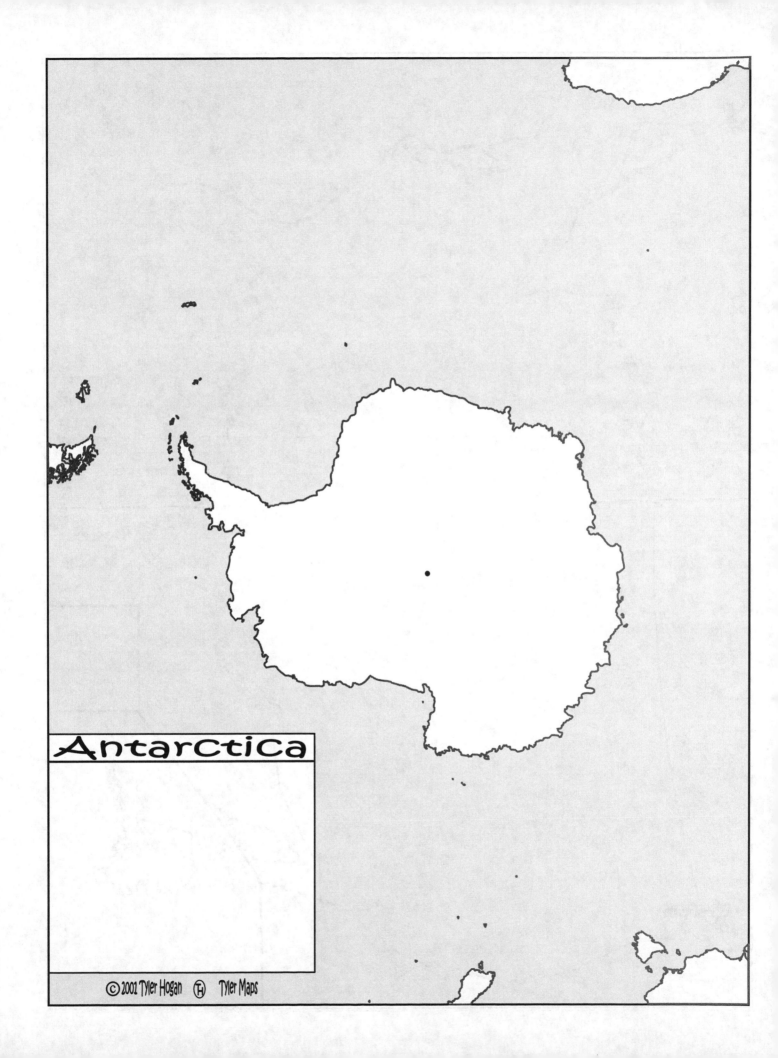

Antarctica

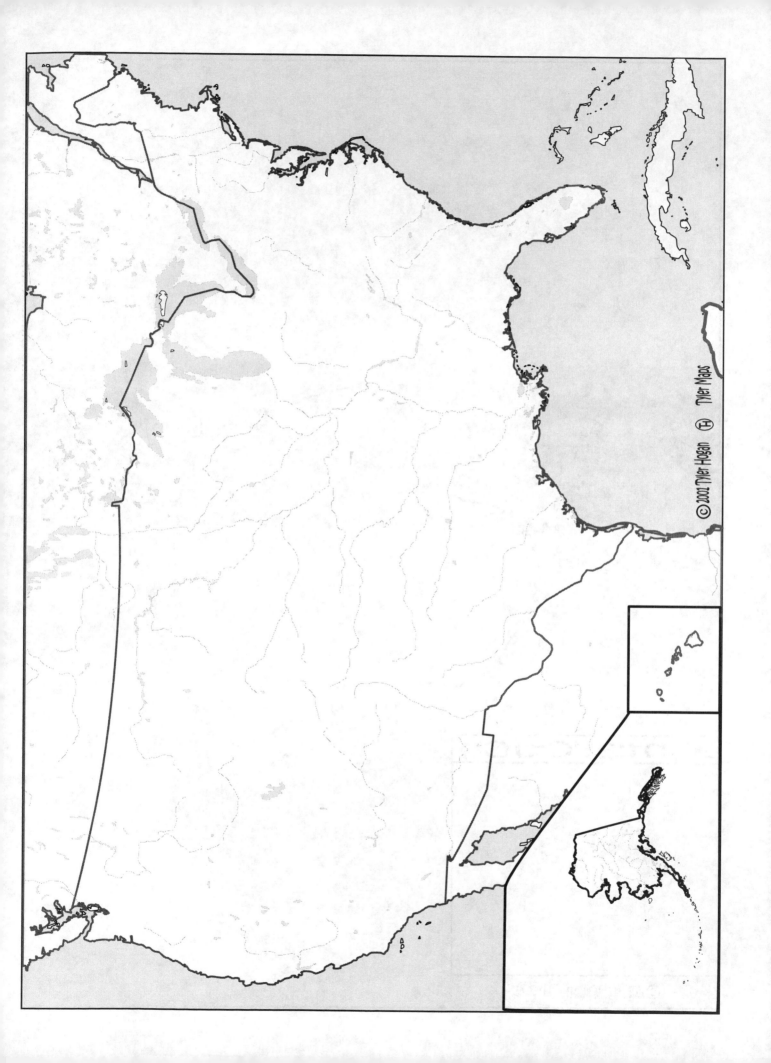

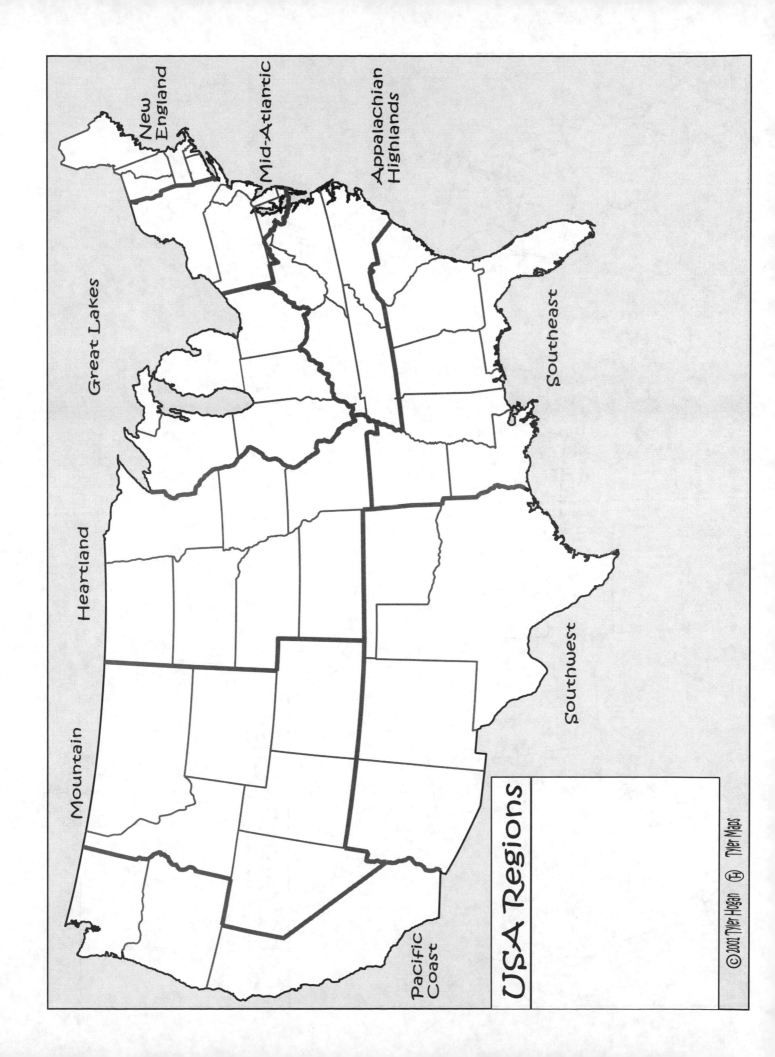

New England

Mid-Atlantic

Appalachian
Highlands

Great Lakes

Southeast

Heartland

Mountain

Southwest

Pacific
Coast

USA Regions

© 2001 Tyler Hogan   Ⓗ   Tyler Maps

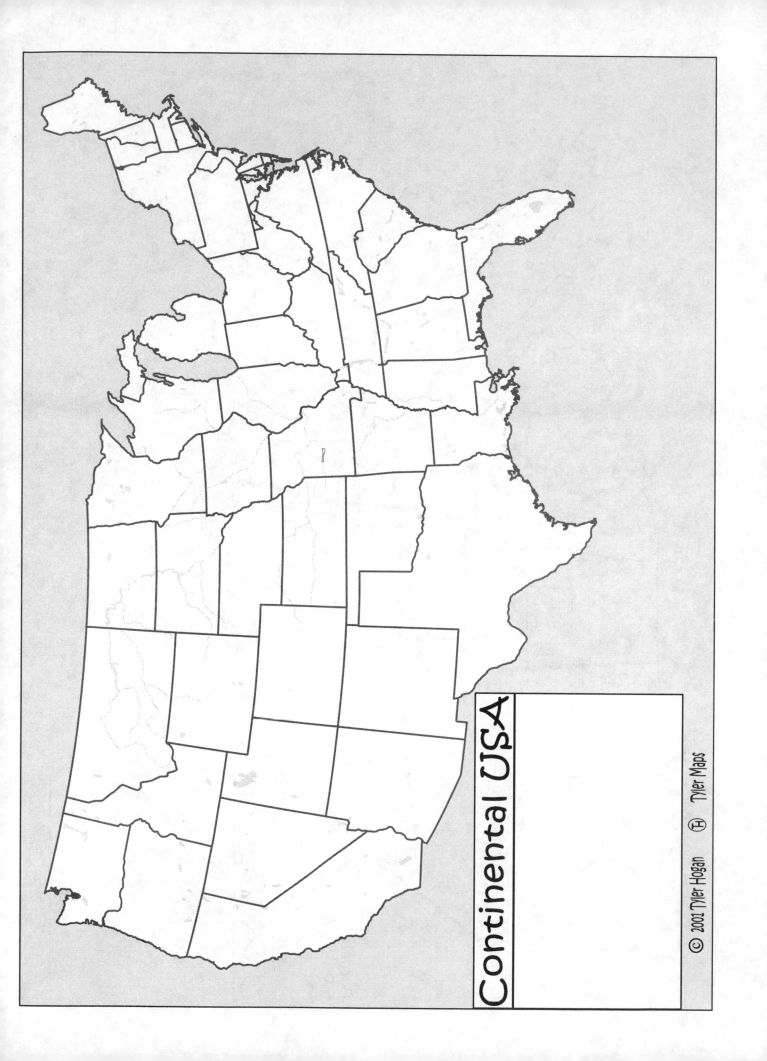

Continental USA

Canada

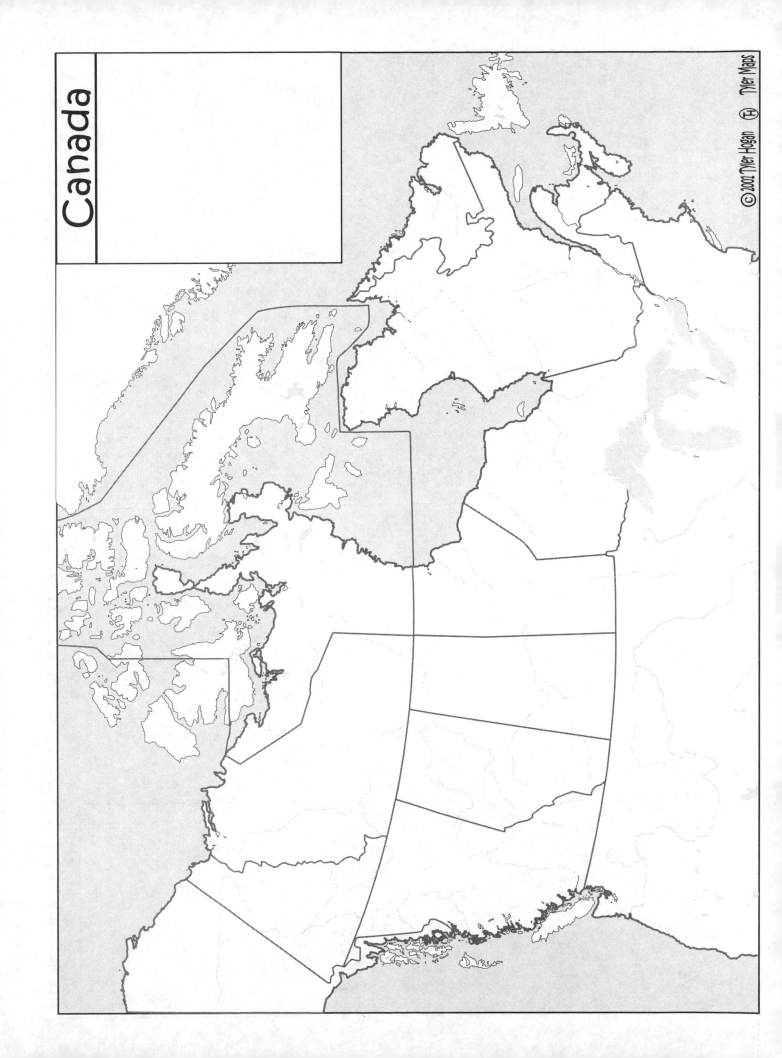

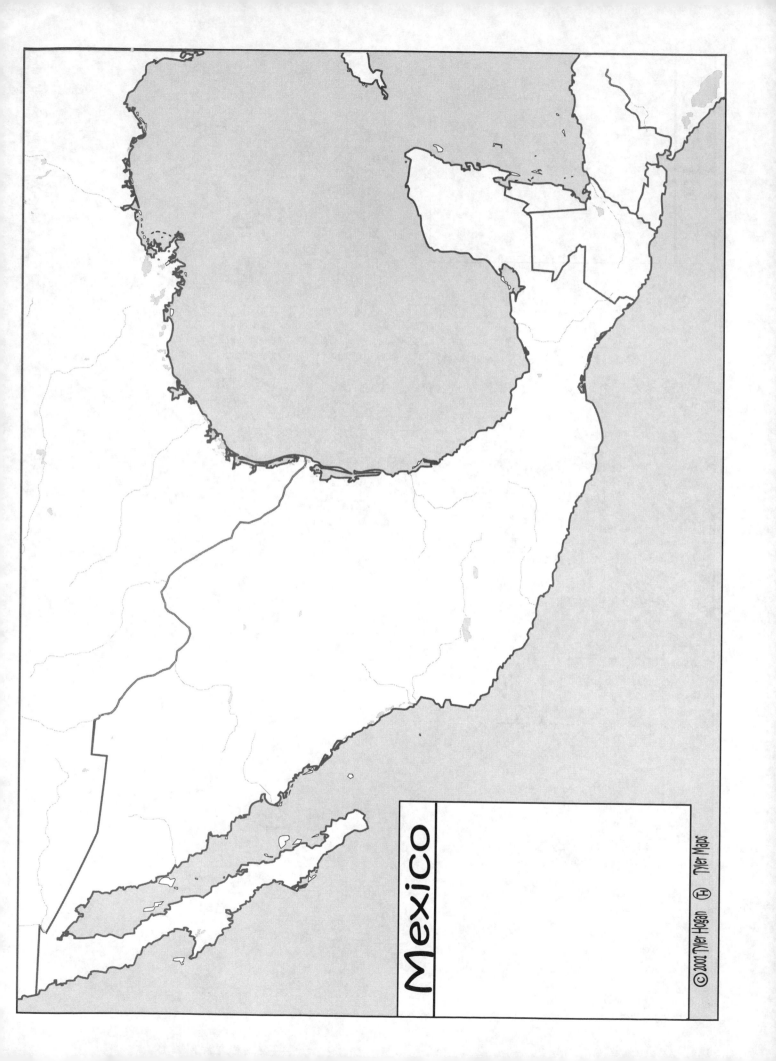

Mexico

Appendix I

Geography in a Flash

"Geography in a Flash"

Included on the Geography in a Flash cards are four USA territories and the 50 states with each state's capital, official bird and flower. *The Volume Library: A Modern, Authoritative Reference for Home and School Use* published by The Southwestern Company was used for the state bird and flower references. (Variations on these may be found, depending upon the reference book used.)

These cards may be used in a number of different ways. Here are three ideas to get you started.

Memory

Materials

- Two sets of copies of all the cards from page 127-135.

You may wish to use the Master Back copy on page 126 to be the back of all the cards. (The cards have been laid out with equal margins on each side of the page. In order to keep the cards aligned, ensure this remains accurate when making copies.) For durability, you may wish to copy onto cardstock and cover with contact paper.

Directions

1. Shuffle both sets of cards.
2. Lay all of them face down in even rows.
3. First player turns over two cards, if they match, i.e., Florida and Florida, he keeps them and turns over two more cards.
4. If the cards don't match, they are placed back in the same position, face down.
5. The next player proceeds in the same manner.
6. A player's turn is over when a match is not made.
7. The object is to collect the most sets of matching cards.

- -

Geography in a Flash Game

Materials

- Two sets of copies of all the cards on pages 127-135.

Important! Before copying -- use Post-it Note™ paper to cover either the state name or the capital name.

"Geography in a Flash" (continued)

Directions

The set with either the state or capital names removed becomes the student set. The teacher set has all the information left intact. Use these cards to quiz the student (or the teacher!).

Use a reward system (stars, pennies, chocolate chips, etc.) for motivation.

- -

USA Mini-Book

Materials

- One set of cards on pages 127-135.
- One set of Master Backs from page 126.

Copy all onto color cardstock.

Directions

1. Cut out the cards.
2. Alphabetize.
3. Place a star on each state to show where the capital is located.
4. Option – write or draw more information on the back of each card: population, famous citizen, state bug, etc.
5. Use a Master Back for both the front and back of the book.
6. Bind.

Geography in a Flash

BRIGHT IDEAS PRESS, INC.

Geography in a Flash

BRIGHT IDEAS PRESS, INC.

Geography in a Flash

BRIGHT IDEAS PRESS, INC.

Geography in a Flash

BRIGHT IDEAS PRESS, INC.

Geography in a Flash

BRIGHT IDEAS PRESS, INC.

Geography in a Flash

BRIGHT IDEAS PRESS, INC.

Alabama

Capital: Montgomery
State Flower: Camellia
State Bird: Yellowhammer

Alaska

Capital: Juneau
State Flower: Forget-me-not
State Bird: Willow Ptarmigan

Arizona

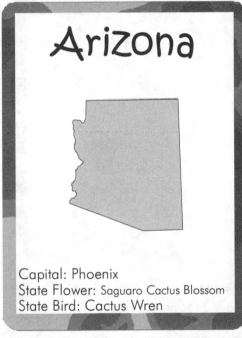

Capital: Phoenix
State Flower: Saguaro Cactus Blossom
State Bird: Cactus Wren

Arkansas

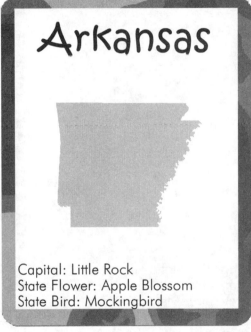

Capital: Little Rock
State Flower: Apple Blossom
State Bird: Mockingbird

California

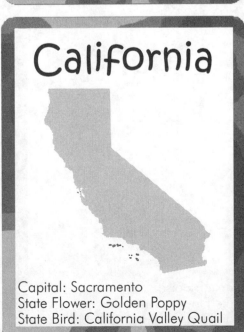

Capital: Sacramento
State Flower: Golden Poppy
State Bird: California Valley Quail

Colorado

Capital: Denver
State Flower: Rocky Mountain Columbine
State Bird: Lark Bunting

Connecticut

Capital: Hartford
State Flower: Mountain Laurel
State Bird: Robin

Delaware

Capital: Dover
State Flower: Peach Blossom
State Bird: Blue Hen Chicken

Florida

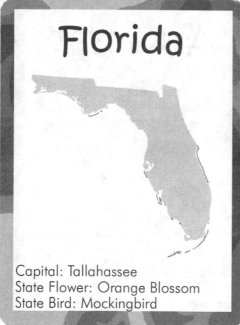

Capital: Tallahassee
State Flower: Orange Blossom
State Bird: Mockingbird

Georgia

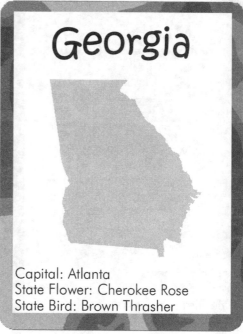

Capital: Atlanta
State Flower: Cherokee Rose
State Bird: Brown Thrasher

Hawaii

Capital: Honolulu
State Flower: Hibiscus
State Bird: Nene (Hawaiian Goose)

Idaho

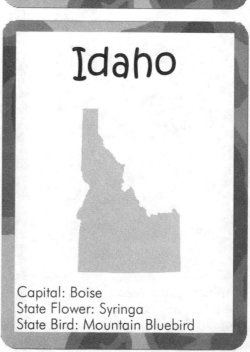

Capital: Boise
State Flower: Syringa
State Bird: Mountain Bluebird

Illinois

Capital: Springfield
State Flower: Native Violet
State Bird: Cardinal

Indiana

Capital: Indianapolis
State Flower: Peony
State Bird: Cardinal

Iowa

Capital: Des Moines
State Flower: Wild Rose
State Bird: Eastern Goldfinch

Kansas

Capital: Topeka
State Flower: Sunflower
State Bird: Western Meadowlark

Kentucky

Capital: Frankfort
State Flower: Goldenrod
State Bird: Cardinal

Louisiana

Capital: Baton Rouge
State Flower: Magnolia
State Bird: Eastern Brown Pelican

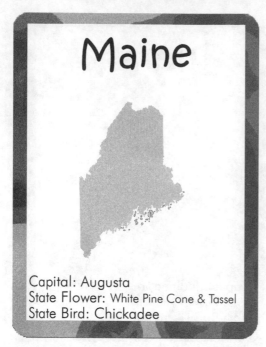

Maine

Capital: Augusta
State Flower: White Pine Cone & Tassel
State Bird: Chickadee

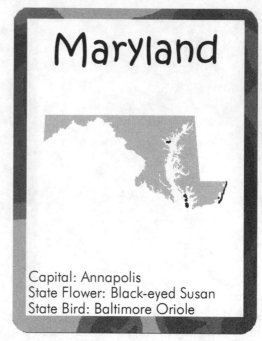

Maryland

Capital: Annapolis
State Flower: Black-eyed Susan
State Bird: Baltimore Oriole

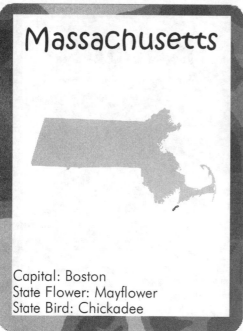

Massachusetts

Capital: Boston
State Flower: Mayflower
State Bird: Chickadee

Michigan

Capital: Lansing
State Flower: Apple Blossom
State Bird: Robin

Minnesota

Capital: St. Paul
State Flower: Pink & White Lady's-Slipper
State Bird: Common Loon

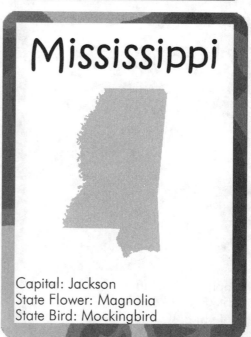

Mississippi

Capital: Jackson
State Flower: Magnolia
State Bird: Mockingbird

Missouri

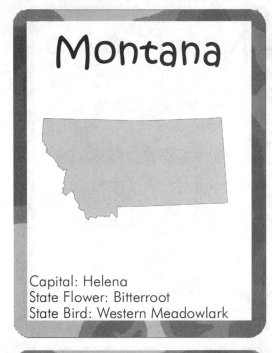

Capital: Jefferson City
State Flower: Hawthorn
State Bird: Bluebird

Montana

Capital: Helena
State Flower: Bitterroot
State Bird: Western Meadowlark

Nebraska

Capital: Lincoln
State Flower: Goldenrod
State Bird: Western Meadowlark

Nevada

Capital: Carson City
State Flower: Sagebrush
State Bird: Mountain Bluebird

New Hampshire

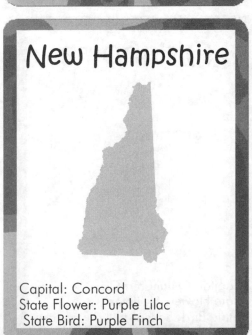

Capital: Concord
State Flower: Purple Lilac
State Bird: Purple Finch

New Jersey

Capital: Trenton
State Flower: Purple Violet
State Bird: Eastern Goldfinch

New Mexico

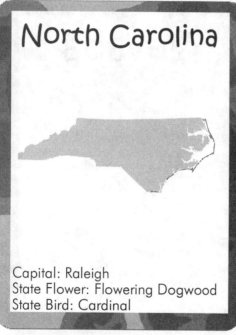

Capital: Santa Fe
State Flower: Yucca
State Bird: Road Runner

New York

Capital: Albany
State Flower: Rose
State Bird: Bluebird

North Carolina

Capital: Raleigh
State Flower: Flowering Dogwood
State Bird: Cardinal

North Dakota

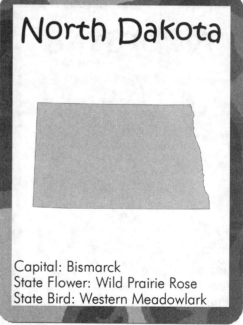

Capital: Bismarck
State Flower: Wild Prairie Rose
State Bird: Western Meadowlark

Ohio

Capital: Columbus
State Flower: Scarlet Carnation
State Bird: Cardinal

Oklahoma

Capital: Oklahoma City
State Flower: Mistletoe
State Bird: Scissor-tailed Flycatcher

Oregon

Capital: Salem
State Flower: Oregon Grape
State Bird: Western Meadowlark

Pennsylvania

Capital: Harrisburg
State Flower: Mountain Laurel
State Bird: Ruffed Grouse

Rhode Island

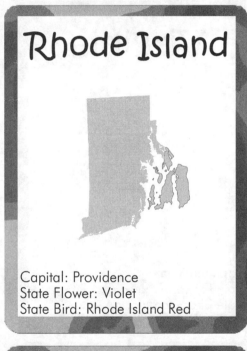

Capital: Providence
State Flower: Violet
State Bird: Rhode Island Red

South Carolina

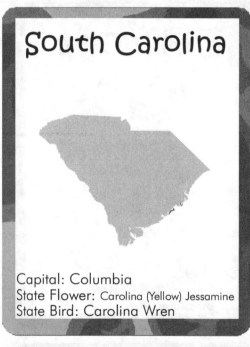

Capital: Columbia
State Flower: Carolina (Yellow) Jessamine
State Bird: Carolina Wren

South Dakota

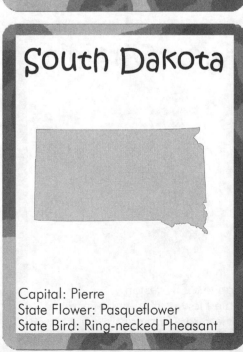

Capital: Pierre
State Flower: Pasqueflower
State Bird: Ring-necked Pheasant

Tennessee

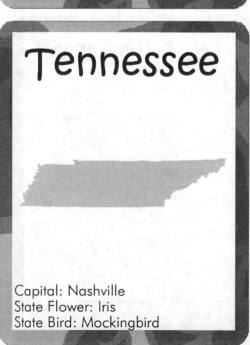

Capital: Nashville
State Flower: Iris
State Bird: Mockingbird

Texas

Capital: Austin
State Flower: Bluebonnet
State Bird: Mockingbird

Utah

Capital: Salt Lake City
State Flower: Sego Lily
State Bird: Sea Gull

Vermont

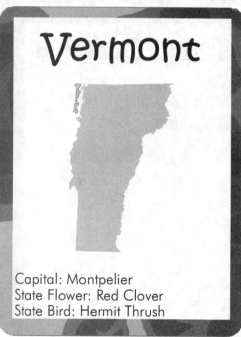

Capital: Montpelier
State Flower: Red Clover
State Bird: Hermit Thrush

Virginia

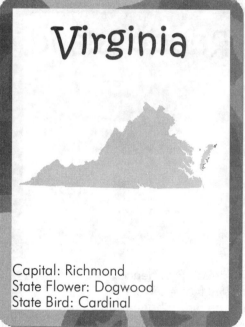

Capital: Richmond
State Flower: Dogwood
State Bird: Cardinal

Washington

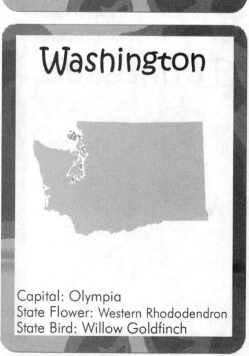

Capital: Olympia
State Flower: Western Rhododendron
State Bird: Willow Goldfinch

West Virginia

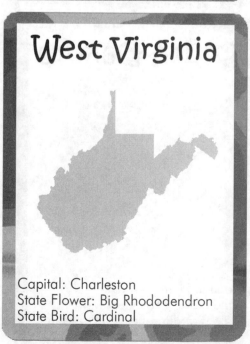

Capital: Charleston
State Flower: Big Rhododendron
State Bird: Cardinal

Wisconsin

Capital: Madison
State Flower: Wood Violet
State Bird: Robin

Wyoming

Capital: Cheyenne
State Flower: Indian Paintbrush
State Bird: Meadowlark

American Samoa

USA Territory
Capital: Pago Pago
People are U.S. Nationals
Language: Samoan and English

Guam

USA Territory
Capital: Agana
People have U.S. Citizenship
Language: English and Chamorro

Puerto Rico

USA Territory
Capital: San Juan
People have U.S. Citizenship
Language: Spanish and English

U.S. Virgin Islands

USA Territory
Capital: Charlotte Amalie
People have U.S. Citizenship
Language: English

Appendix II

Geography Resources

Geography Resources

Places to Write

LINK International
This terrific newsletter is published by *Voice of the Martyrs*. Great for current events, geography, history, Bible and prayer life! Free -- donations accepted.
P.O. Box 443
Bartlesville, OK 74005-9934

The Imagination Team
Bureau of Land Management
Anasazi Heritage Center
27501 Highway 184 Box 758
Dolores, CO 81323

Going for the Gold -- colorful poster: history of gold and geological information. $1.50

National Geographic Society
1145 17th Street NW
Washington, DC 20036-4688

Write for information about the Geography Bee. (See page 2.)

U.S. Geological Survey (USGS)
USGS Information Services
Box 25286
Denver, CO 80225
888.ASK-USGS

www.usgs.gov/education/edulist.html
One of their free books is *Volcanoes of the United States*.
Write and ask about being a volunteer in the Earth Science Corps -- in which private citizens can participate in updating map information in their area. They also have a catalog of maps available for sale.

Prayer Point
P.O. Box 3000
Boone, NC 28607-3000

www.samaritanspurse.org
Subscribe to their free newsletter -- great for current events. Learn about "Operation Christmas Child."

Geography Resources (continued)

United States Capitol Historical Society
200 Maryland Avenue NE
Washington, DC 20002

Ask for your free fact sheet describing the history of the United States Capitol Building, which houses congress. For under five dollars you may purchase the book, The Flag of the United States, an excellent resource about the history of our flag as well as state flags, seals, and mottoes. For the free fact sheet send a self-addressed, stamped business-size envelope. Ask for the current price of the flag book.

The Statue of Liberty -- Ellis Island Foundation
Office of Public Affairs
52 Vanderbilt Avenue
New York, NY 10017
Send a $3.00 check to obtain fact sheets and coloring pages about America's immigrant history.

National Archives and Records Administration
Publications Distribution
Room G9
Seventh Street and Pennsylvania Ave. N.W.
Washington, DC 20408
800.234.8861

The National Archives and Records Administration offers a free genealogy packet.

Web Sites

www.nationalgeographic.com/education

Created specifically for teachers and students this site has online adventures with world-famous explorers, maps and geography information, lesson plans, a teacher forum and store. Great site!

---

www.ed.gov/pubs/parents/geography/index.html

This web site has a nice geography booklet for children that you can print out. By backing up into the main menu you can find out about other available publications.

Geography Resources (continued)

http://ericir.syr.edu/

The ERIC Digest is a granddaddy of educational resources. You can get lost in here looking for articles, lesson plans, etc., submitted by teachers and researchers from all over the country. (Be discerning.)

_____

www.nara.gov

You can visit the National Archives and Records Administration at their web site for interesting information and lesson plans.

_____

www.angelfire.com/mo/sasschool/ArtQuest.html

History and geography through art -- lesson plans and resources on-line.

_____

http://spaceplace.jpl.nasa.gov

The NASA Space Place provides interesting facts, fun activities and exciting contests for students in grades K-6.

_____

www.homeschoolingusa.com

Kiko is a site filled with free Internet lessons on every subject imaginable.

_____

eNature.com

This site features searchable field guides to more than 4,800 plants and animals in North America! Also includes teacher tips, on-line naturalists, message boards and e-newsletters.

Geography Resources (continued)

Other

Check with your local Chamber of Commerce to get free maps of your area. When traveling, contact Chambers of Commerce or State Departments of Tourism ahead of time to get maps of places you will be visiting. Your librarian should be able to help you find reference books with these addresses.

The United States Post Office is a great place for free materials. Ask for Publication 39 -- a free stamp coloring book. Many other terrific booklets on stamps and stamp collecting are available there.

The American Red Cross is a wealth of useful and free materials. We've gotten everything from a blood-typing kit to disaster-preparedness coloring books. Check out yours today! Many items are produced by NOAA. Look for the free booklet *Owlie Skywarn's Weather Book* and many others.

Materials and Curriculum

Bright Ideas Press
P.O. Box 333
Cheswold, DE 19936
877.492.8081
www.BrightIdeasPress.com
Your source for maps, timelines, *Hands-On Geography*, and many other geography, science, and history books and resources. Here is just a small sample of what Bright Ideas Press carries:

The Ultimate Geography and Timeline Guide, $34.95, K-12
Whether you are a unit study or textbook fan, you'll find much to love about this award winning curriculum guide! This non-consumable book will be your mainstay all the way through high school and is especially good for teaching a wide variety of ages together. Includes lesson plans and suggestions for teaching geography through American history, literature, science, math, and the Interne; as well as fun and games, reproducible activity sheets, scope and sequence, and tons of teaching ideas! A full section is devoted to timelines and even includes 340 reproducible historical timeline figures. Indexed.

The Student History Notebook of America, $12.95, K-12
The student notebook approach to learning is flexible, interesting, and memorable! Witness improvements in the quality of students' work as they record information, artwork, daily assignments, etc. in their own personal notebook. Includes pages for essays, drawings, vocabulary, presidents, states and capitals, and much more. The timeline and ten outline maps contribute depth as well as hands-on learning. Works great for a 50 state study as well.

Geography Resources (continued)

Over Our Heads in Wonder - Science & the Sky, $9.95, K-5
Your Sourcebook for Bible Devotions with Science Experiments! With 25 Readings/Discussions and 50+ Activities/experiments encompassing science, Bible, writing, math, reading, art, and research, there is no shortage of ideas here! Suitable for multi-level teaching, these "any day -- anywhere" activities utilize common household materials and are organized around the different facets of weather and the sky: clouds, rainbows, sun, stars, snow, wind, storms, and air. A gem of a book!

Laminated Cloud Chart
This colorful poster is as beautiful as it is useful! Identify and name clouds with the labeled color photographs. Comes with an additional black and white chart of forecast rules -- after you identify the cloud, forecast the weather! A must for any weather unit in science or geography.

The Scientist's Apprentice, $26.95, K-6
This exciting, complete one-year science curriculum is presented in an easily understandable manner and is just as easy to use. Experiments, games, crafts, recipes, writing, songs and more are then creatively integrated to reach a variety of learning styles. Orderly thinking skills (based on the scientific method) are reinforced throughout. Bonus -- 3 of the 4 included topics encompass geography as well as science! Four 8 week units: Astronomy, Earth Science, Oceanography, and Anatomy. Suitable for multi-level teaching grades K-6.

Atlases
A variety of atlases are a must for any geography study and especially for the National Geography Bee preparation. The Classroom and Answer Atlases are both filled with good information in an easy-to-read format.
Classroom Atlas -- recommended for elementary and middle school. $9.95
Answer Atlas -- recommended for upper middle and high school. $12.95

Historical Atlases - ideal for all studies. Call for catalog or check out our web site.

Laminated Mark-It Outline Maps
These are maps to write-on and wipe-off. Perfect for hands-on learning. Variety of maps. Prices range from $6.95 to $10.95. Call for details. Beautiful and up-to-date Reference Maps also available.

See you at The Bee!

BRIGHT IDEAS PRESS
www.BrightIdeasPress.com

ORDER FORM

Order on-line:
www.brightideaspress.com

Or mail this form with your check or money order to:
Bright Ideas Press
P.O. Box 333
Cheswold, DE 19936
Toll Free: 877.492.8081

SHIPPING TABLE

Up to $60..................…..6.00
$61-$150..................….......10%
Over $150..................…...FREE

Most orders are shipped within 4 business days.

ITEM #	TITLE	QTY	PRICE	TOTAL
BIP-1	Hands-On Geography		$ 14.95	
BIP-2	The Scientist's Apprentice		$ 26.95	
BIP-3	Student History Notebook of America		$ 12.95	
BIP-4	Over Our Heads In Wonder		$ 9.95	
BIP-5	The Mystery of History Volume 1		$ 44.95	
BIP-6	Christian Kids Explore Biology		$ 29.95	
BIP-7	The Mystery of History Volume 2		$ 44.95	
BIP-8	Christian Kids Explore Chemistry		$ 29.95	
BIP-9	Christian Kids Explore Earth & Space		$ 29.95	
GG-102	Gifted Children at Home		$ 24.95	
GC-100	The Ultimate Geography and Timeline Guide		$ 34.95	
BIP-10	All American History Volume 1			
BIP-11	Basic to Baghdad – A Soldier Writes Home			

SHIP TO ADDRESS: Please print clearly.

NAME:_____

ADDRESS:_____

_____

_____

PHONE: (____)_____

EMAIL:_____

Special!!!
FREE SHIPPING
on orders
over $150.00

Subtotal	
←**Shipping Cost:** See Shipping Table	
Total Amount Due	

Credit Card Information

VISA/MasterCard Number   Exp. Date

Signature

Practical, Fun and Affordable Geography, History and Science Resources!